YOLO
You Only Lead One

**8 Principles for Leading Yourself
Before You Lead Others**

Jonathan M. Leath

Printed in the United States of America
2019 First Edition
10 9 8 7 6 5 4 3 2 1

Subject Index:
Leath, Jonathan M.
Title: You Only Lead One: 8 Principles for Leading Yourself Before You Lead Others
1. Leadership 2. Relationships 3. Inspirational 4. Motivational Leadership 5.Anabolic Energy 6. Self-Awareness 7. Emotional Intelligence 8. Cultural Intelligence

Library of Congress Card Catalog Number: 2019918475
Paperback ISBN: 978-0-578-59579-5

Leath & Associates LLC
jonathanleath.com

PRAISES FOR YOLO LEADERSHIP...

"Pastor Jonathan has developed a fantastic blueprint for self-leadership. If you want your inner circle and team to grow, you must develop yourself. In *YOLO: You Only Lead One*, you will find an intentional walk across the thoughts of great human behaviorists and psychologists that reminds us of how we think about ourselves and others. Pastor Jonathan challenges us to enter into the journey of self-awareness and self-control so we can examine our strengths and vulnerabilities to become better leaders. He provides tools for self-assessment and tips for understanding the YOLO leadership premise. Pastor Jonathan calls us to action by encouraging us to know ourselves deeply, to know the impact of our behaviors on ourselves and on others. He shares what successful leaders understand; that they must master every single aspect of who they are and leave behind every excuse that hinders their personal growth and success. This book will excite you, challenge you, and set you up to move into your next level of leadership."

Ana I. Berdecia, M.Ed., Certified Life & Leadership Coach & CEO Potential Pathways, LLC

Co-author, *Discover Your Team's Potential Proven Principles to Help Engage Your Team & Improve Performance*

"Pastor Jonathan knocks it out of the ballpark! If you want to lead others well, you must first lead yourself. Self-mastery is the key to dynamic personal growth and lasting success in life."

George Bowen, Co-Pastor Converge (formerly Maranatha Christian Fellowship)

"Mastering one's emotions is a key driver for managing life's complex situations and winning in relationships. YOLO provides a simple yet provocative framework for us to assess, activate, and achieve that mastery.

Vaughn L. McKoy, JD, MBA

"As a leader, one of the hardest tasks we encounter is the art of leading ourselves in our personal and professional life. Jonathan Leath demonstrates the clear and present challenges of trying to effectively lead others without a solid self-awareness foundation as our guide. In *YOLO: 8 Principles for Leading Yourself Before You Lead Others*, we are given thought-provoking tools and strategies to embark upon an honest, transparent, journey to master self-control and lead yourself. *YOLO* is a great resource for anyone seeking a new approach to personal growth development."

Rev. Dr. Elliott H Johnson Sr
Heyward and Johnson LLC

"Philippians 2:4 reminds us to " Look not every man on his own things, but every man also on the things of others." I think of Pastor Leath when I read this verse. One of the reasons he is a leader is because he cares about others. He cares about others to the point that he is sharing what he has learned and what we need to know about ourselves before we can lead others. I am honored to endorse his new book, *You Only Lead One.* Congratulations, Pastor Leath, on your new book! May God continue to bless you abundantly!"

Claudia Hawkins, Ethics Training and Consulting, LLC

"The premise of YOLO engages an important and necessary topic at the heart of mankind. In a culture that praises power, Jonathan reminds us that true staying power is found in understanding and leading oneself first, before leading others. I am excited about the impact this book will have on anyone who lays their hands on it!"

Peter Abungu
Founder and CEO, Swahiba Networks, Nairobi, Kenya

"I have spent years studying leadership as an academic in the throes of a doctoral dissertation to praxis as the front-line leader of a fledgling non-profit organization. Effective leadership is hard work, no matter from which angle it is examined. With his YOLO framework, Jonathan Leath strikes at the very heart of why leadership is difficult—because we must do the difficult work of transforming deficits in our internal selves before we earn the character and social capital to successfully guide others towards transformational change. Using his own challenging pastoral experiences as a backdrop, the author deftly models the authenticity that he advocates for all of us who desire to leave the world better than we found it."

Dr. Harold Arnold Jr., President of Eusebeia, Inc, and author of *The Unfair Advantage: A Grace-inspired Path to Winning at Marriage*

"I met Jonathan Leath twenty plus years ago when he "came a courtin" a lovely young lady attending Agape in Rahway, New Jersey. Kamili wanted her pastor to check him out and comment. I was delighted to do so, and thankfully he passed the test with flying colors. From the start, I found Jonathan to be an exceptional young man with clear leadership capacity and potential. His knowledge, experience, character, and patent integrity well qualify him to discuss the content presented in this book. If you're serious about leadership development, I strongly encourage you to read YOLO and apply the principles shared. You'll be a better leader—of yourself and others.

Dr. Lawrence Powell

Agape Family Worship Center | www.agapecenter.org

"YOLO is a practical guide to individual leadership as the precursor to successful corporate leadership. Jonathan tackles complex concepts and using a wonderful blend of research and experience, and he provides tangible steps we can all apply to our leadership walk. As a Christian working in a secular leadership position, I appreciate that this book addresses leadership both very important aspects of my life. Thank you for reminding us all that leadership development begins first with ourselves!"

Scott P. McCartney, Ed. D.

Superintendent of Schools

"As an advocate for personal image, I stress the importance of a holistic approach to developing your inner self to present your outward appearance to the world. YOLO is a testament to the fact that self-control and self-awareness go hand-in-hand in your personal growth and development when leading yourself. After reading this book, everyone should be on a journey toward YOLO Leadership, which will build stronger relationships and positive outcomes for the future."

Dr. Alex Ellis
Founder, Tied To Greatness

"YOLO is a must-read guide for existing and aspirational leaders. It's a great tool to help you sharpen your leadership saw. Jonathan paints a fresh picture of what it means to be an effective leader. He provides practical insights and strategies to help you become exceptional at bringing out the best in others by first understanding what it means to lead yourself. He intertwines foundational leadership principles with new concepts that will allow you to make a paradigm shift in how you fulfill your goals by becoming a more impactful leader. "

Jeffrey D. Hatchell
Author of *The Inspired Career - Breathe New Life Into Your Job and Get Equipped, Empowered, & Engaged*!

DEDICATION

This book is dedicated to the four greatest future leaders in the world, my children, Jael, Jonathan, Joshua, and Joel. Thank you for letting me hone my leadership skills on you.

To my wife, Kamili. You are the catalyst who helps me be not only a great leader but a great person. Thank you for joining me on my journey of becoming a YOLO Leader. You definitely play the role of a few of the "7 people" that I need in my life.

ACKNOWLEDGMENTS

Have you ever wanted to do something for a long time? You know, something that you really wanted to accomplish? Well, this is how I felt about this book. For years, I have wanted to be an author but didn't know how to do it. This book you are holding has literally been 20 years in the making. Little did I know that a boy who grew up on a dirt road in Elon, North Carolina, who primed tobacco in the summer and raised pigs in the winter, could ever accomplish the things that I have been able to accomplish.

It all started with a dream. There is nothing special about me. I am an ordinary man who wants to make a difference in this world. Today my dream has become a reality, and this book is proof that with the right people in your life, you can achieve all that you set out to accomplish. Keep God first and treat others right, and the sky is the limit.

I first want to thank my wife, Kamili, for giving me the freedom to follow and pursue every idea, dream, plan, and whim that I have. You are truly one of the "7 People I Need in My Life."

I also want to thank my four wonderful children: Jael–my *creative*, Jonathan–my *analytic*, Joshua–my *competitive,* and Joel–my *energetic*!

Additionally, I want to thank a few of the greatest leaders I know: The late Apostle Otis Lockett, Sr., Bishop C. Milton Grannum and Dr. Lawrence R. Powell, the late Mr. & Mrs. David, and Annie Simpson - these remarkable people helped me hone my leadership skills and to develop me as a leader.

Thank you to all of my Destiny Family Worship Center members – formerly Destiny Church (past and present) – no journey is a straight line. I appreciate all of the support and love you showed me. To my new Converge Church family, I look forward to the journey we have just begun.

Special shout outs to the people who continually sharpen me as a leader: Julius Koonce, Samuel E. Ponder, Michael A. Brunson, Reginald Holiday, John Lofton, Keith Wilks, Sr., Darrell & Lakisha Williams, Chip Rice, Michael & Whanita Sudler, Karla Wright Leath, George & Thelma Patrick, and George Bowen. Kim Rouse, my amazing book coach, who not only pushed me to complete this book but rolled up her sleeves to help me complete it.

Finally, thank you to my parents: Donald and Ruthie *– for giving me physical life* and my siblings and their spouses: DJ, Andre (Charlene), Boris (Nancia), and Christie (Sam) *– for not taking that life when we were children (it's a long story)!*

I hope you have as much joy in reading and applying this book to your life and leadership as I have in writing it.

Jonathan M. Leath – #YOLO LEADER

TABLE OF CONTENTS

FOREWORD

With a vast majority of leadership books focused on the external – execution, strategy, performance, profit, and growth, my friend, Jonathan Leath, bravely focuses on the hardest part of leadership, and that is the leadership of one's self. As Jonathan says, in his transformational book, *You Only Lead One: 8 Principles for Leading Yourself Before You Lead Others* (YOLO), to lead yourself, you must first know yourself.

In reading the manuscript, you, as a reader, quickly learn that Jonathan has experienced faltering as a leader. His willingness to be vulnerable and transparent allowed me to hear his heart and made me want to read more. It has been through his challenges that Jonathan began to learn how to lead himself. I am convinced that it is impossible for a leader to know themselves without faltering and failing along the leadership journey. Yet, instead of dropping out of the race, Jonathan embraced the resilience to stay the course and share his lessons and insights with all of us.

The ANABOLIC leadership acrostic provides a memorable yet straightforward way to integrate the leadership principles into your life. Each chapter concludes with coaching tips for immediate application. These principles are designed to help leaders live, love, and lead well and leave a legacy of profound impact because self-leadership precedes everything. Jonathan understands that it takes a healthy "me" to be a strong "we."

Leadership is hard work, heart work, worth the work, and *You Only Lead One* will help you do the work.

Dr. Johnny Parker

Former Chaplain of the Washington Redskins

Adjunct Professor, Johns Hopkins University

Author of *Turn the Page: Unlocking the Story Within You*

"Leadership, for the most part, is not really about leading a team, a group, a department or a company– it's really about leading yourself."
- Jonathan Leath

PREFACE

As a husband, father, leader, and pastor, *YOLO (You Only Lead One)* has been a recurring thought in my head for many years. I have studied leadership from the position of leading others for over two decades, and a great deal of emphasis is placed on casting vision, forming teams, dealing with conflict, and managing change. While all of these are necessary and are everyday challenges all leaders face, real leadership development starts internally with the sole leader—not with his or her team.

Let's face it; leaders wear several hats: as a vision caster, a team leader, a conflict management specialist, and change agent. We all know that in practice, leading a team, a family, an organization, or a ministry can be overwhelming. When you add managing budgets, overhead, policies and procedures, payroll, and unexpected events, it's no wonder people choose to either abdicate their leadership responsibilities or remain stagnant or mediocre at best.

Being a YOLO leader is not a fad or temporary fix to achieving my goals. It is how I choose to live my life. The YOLO concept became real to me in April 2012 when I had a "church split." For those of you that are not familiar with the term, a church split is when members of a church, usually someone from the leadership team, persuades others to leave the church to start their own or go to another church altogether. I experienced one of the most excruciating, heart-wrenching, leadership testing, and emotionally unsettling events of my life. Facing the reality that the people I had prayed for, prayed over, spent time with, and even cried for, decided that my leadership was not enough. It made me question everything I thought I knew about leadership or whether or not I was supposed to lead at all. You see, when things like this happen, you begin to question who you are, and it shakes you to the core.

I have been involved in leadership for decades but never at the helm. Leading as the second in command did not give me a full grasp of the weight of leadership. Of course, leadership has, in its very nature, a significant responsibility. You get applauded when things go right and blamed when things go wrong. I know firsthand what it's like to be on the receiving end of both. It was at this devastating time in my life and career that I realized that above all else, I *had* to be a YOLO leader. I had to be more self-aware of my actions and inaction. I had to exert more self-control over *every* area of my life. Yes, there are things that I wish I could have done differently, and life is not perfect, but I thank God, my family, and my church, landed on our feet.

A large part of winning at self-control is not only to make better choices but to develop better habits in big things and little things. For example, immediately after church ends on Sunday, I take off my church clothes and put everything on its hanger. It's how I move from one part of my day to the next. If anything, it relaxes my mind and allows me to shift from Pastor Jonathan to daddy. I know it's a small thing, but little things have a high impact on future behavior. I wonder if I'm the only one who gets annoyed when someone doesn't put their shopping cart back in the corral? If we all just stopped for a minute in our daily routines to think about our actions and inactions, we would see what we could have done differently. It's a matter of leaving this world a little bit better than when you found it. Again, small things make a high impact.

At the foundation of a YOLO leader's actions is self-control—the ability to master yourself from within. The Apostle Paul tells us that all things are permissible but not beneficial. [1] Years ago, I was studying Biblical principles and discipline. That's when the words "self-control" began to resonate with me. There is a genuine spiritual principle on how to lead yourself. Why is self-control so challenging for *all* of us? The Bible states that a man without self-control is like a city broken into and left without walls. [2] Who knows? Maybe we are looking at leadership all wrong? Should we be looking at it from the inside out instead of outside in? We live in a world where everyone is fixated on the exterior. So much work goes into looking the part in person, especially on social media. Countless people of all races, ethnicities, religions, and gender are falling due to a lack of self-control. The question remains, how can I help? What can I do to shift the tide? Even if I only help a few, my commitment and passion for spreading the message of self-control remain the same.

My trajectory became motivational speaking. How could I motivate people to live better behind closed doors? Most public failures happened in private first. By the same token, most public victories were already won in secret. Yet after exhaustive efforts motivating others, I realized that motivation wears off after a while. It's like a drug, and you become addicted, needing just one more hit. You hope that the next hit is more powerful than the last.

Similarly, people are addicted to motivation, and they need outside stimulation to get them from one moment to the next. You know them, or you may be one of them: you start off reading a self-help book, then you go to a conference, later you watch YouTube videos or listen to messages in your car or call your life coach. Yet despite your efforts, you still need more. What's the point of making a consistent effort to hear positive messages but never change on the inside? You can't expect a bucket with holes to carry water. There has to be something inside of you that not only motivates you to control yourself but is strong enough to sustain you for months at a time.

"Motivation is the external fuel that feeds your fire to complete the task, while inspiration is the internal fuel that feeds your fire, which won't stop burning until you complete the task."

Motivation vs Inspiration

The YOLO leader is *internally driven* rather than *externally pulled*. Billions of dollars are spent on motivating people. **Motivated** people will give you the immediate results you desire but **Inspired** people will help develop the people around them while getting those desired results.

Old Leadership Model

Requires immediate reward when task is completed

"I listen to **WHFM**"
(What's In It For Me)

Needs
constant
reminders
of end
goal
(*What*)

Task Orented

Will get results
you need

The Motivated Leader
("Motive"or "Reason")
Outward Focused and **Externally Pulled**

Motivation vs Inspiration

The YOLO leader is *internally driven* rather than *externally pulled.* Billions of dollars are spent on motivating people. **Motivated** people will give you the immediate results you desire but **Inspired** people will help develop the people around them while getting those desired results.

YOLO Leadership Model

Can wait for reward

Needs Clear Vision, few reminders (Why)

Will develop the people him

Goal focused

" I Listen to **WIIFW"** (What's In It For We)

The Inspired Leader
("In Spirit or Divine Guidance")
Outward Focused and **Internally Driven**

I believe that each leader needs to live at a higher moral standard than the previous leader to influence the next generation. As a Christian in Corporate America, I decided to integrate my life. I wasn't smart enough to keep up the facade of being two different people: Jonathan at work and Jonathan at church. I chose to be the same, no matter the environment. I recall a meeting with the late Dr. Myles Munroe, at a leadership conference in Plainfield, New Jersey, where I asked him what does it mean to have integrity? He replied, "When you are a person of integrity, it means that you have integrated your life."

With an intentional approach to YOLO leadership, we can take all of these components and boil them down to one simple idea...You Only Lead One! The YOLO principle suggests that each person in every role and every function must become responsible for leading themselves. We cannot multitask with this life-changing concept. It must be practiced and mastered. It is a scientifically proven fact that humans cannot multitask effectively.[3] When the brain tries to do two things at once, it divides and conquers, so we are undertaking a task at half capacity.[4] I watch Good Morning America, and they cram so much information into the screen simultaneously, and no matter how hard I try to read the bottom ticker, listen, and watch, the information overload is impossible to comprehend. We have to focus on one thing at a time.

There are some things that I still struggle with but as a YOLO Leader I have adopted this ANABOLIC leadership model of eight principles which provides an understanding of exceptional leadership qualities to help reprogram my brain: **A**= Authentic, **N**= Nice, **A**= Accurate, **B**= Brilliant, **O**= Objective and Open-minded, **L**= Lead with Love, **I**= Integrated and **C**= Character. So whether you're a pastor, business owner, housewife, student, corporate executive, stay at home mom, or whatever state you are in, you have to learn that the greatest lesson of leadership is to lead yourself first.

In this book, we will look at how self-mastery in each of the eight ANABOLIC principles will help you develop a solid personal leadership foundation on which you can build stronger. I certainly don't have all the answers, but I do know that each person can be responsible for their own personal level of self-control and awareness. If you can master and control your private life by leading yourself from the inside out, you reap the benefits of great character, integrity, and peace in your public life. Striving to become a YOLO leader is a mindset shift and intentional step in your life that is truly priceless.

Jonathan M. Leath

*"If you do not conquer self,
you will be conquered by self."*

- Napoleon Hill

PART I

YOLO Discovery

*"Self-awareness sets you
on a path to success."*

CHAPTER 1

SELF-AWARENESS

What does it mean to find oneself? Are we all lost in a never-ending cycle of uncertainty and fear? I've heard people say, "I just need to find myself," yet I'm not sure if they are sincere or just using it as a way to avoid dealing with a challenging or uncomfortable situation. The key to finding yourself is to tap into your self-awareness perception. Self-awareness, in a nutshell, is having a keen awareness of your one and only unique self. What makes you happy? Sad? Emotional? Angry? Fulfilled? In other words, knowing your key triggers will allow you to handle various circumstances better.

Finding yourself requires a careful, honest self-evaluation of your personality, which includes your strengths, weaknesses, thoughts, beliefs, motivation, and emotions.

Equally important is that you will see an added benefit to your self-searching process, becoming more in tune with how others perceive you. Intentional self-awareness creates the opportunity to make changes in your behavior and beliefs immediately since self-awareness comes from experiences. Every encounter that you have, whether good, bad, or indifferent, your mind provides an interpretation of that experience going forward and creates a pattern for handling it. With practice, you have the opportunity to change unfavorable habits into more attractive ones that will be beneficial to you and may lead to behaviors that others will follow.

Back to Basics

If you're going to become YOLO Leaders, you've got to go back to when you first became aware of yourselves. A lot of times, our self-awareness, that initial stage will determine the level or amount of work that we have to do now to become a YOLO leader in the future. If we can't pinpoint a time when we became self-aware, it will be challenging to lead ourselves. Unfortunately, many people still haven't found themselves regardless of their age or experiences. Therefore, commit to putting a stake in the ground and use some of the tools discussed in this book to start your self-awareness journey.

I was an adjunct professor at Pneuma Life School of Ministry in Rahway, New Jersey. I taught some of the significant theories of personality development in a class that was designed by Oral Roberts University. My course on Faith and Human Development provided students with insight into the

3

leading self-awareness theorists. One of the most well-known names is Sigmund Freud, known for the tripartite Id, Ego, and Superego psyche theories.[5] The Id is the source of a person's drives and impulses. It is concerned with immediate gratification (food, sex, and comfort). Next, the Ego which is the source of our rational or reality-oriented functions. This is where we have a sense of our reality with what is real, and we learn what is capable. The Ego is also where we develop our secondary process of thinking, and we take in the possibilities of what things can and cannot be. Finally, the Superego is our conscious, moral, or ethical sense. This is where we derive our social, moral, and ethical restraints. Superego is often revealed in conversations when something atrocious happens, and we say, "How could a person do that?" According to Freud, it's in the Superego that we verbally express something as being morally reprehensible—where we draw the line.[6]

The next theorist of the personality concept was introduced by Erik Erikson, a German-American psychologist, in what he describes as the Eight Stages of Psychosocial Development. Erikson builds on the Ego concept of Freud by emphasizing the social environment rather than erotic or self-gratification. Erikson's theory stresses the person's rational and social capabilities and development is understood only in the context of society and culture.[7] Therefore, Erikson's findings conclude that you determine who you are based on your culture. In other words, any of your setbacks, challenges, or fears are based upon your cultural norms. This point is brought home by Pastor Keith Scazzero in *Emotionally Healthy Spirituality*, when he writes, "You may have God in your heart, but you got grandpa in your bones." Again, the culture you grow up in has long-term effects on you.

Erikson assigns Eight Stages to your personality realization. Failure to master these tasks can lead to feelings of inadequacy.

Stage #1: Trust vs. Mistrust

Birth to 12 months old: At this early age, babies learn to trust adults to meet their basic needs for survival. Parents who respond to their baby's needs help the child develop a sense of trust so that the child views the environment as a safe, predictable space. On the flip side, if babies are not nurtured, they are likely to grow up with anxiety and mistrust people.

Stage #2 Autonomy vs. Shame/Doubt

Ages 1-3: Toddlers learn to explore their surroundings and act in their environment to get results. They begin to discover their likes and dislikes as it relates to food, clothing, and toys, as well as resolving the conflict of autonomy versus shame and doubt, as they work to establish independence. This is what's called the "me do it" stage.

Stage #3 Initiative vs. Guilt

Ages 3-6: Preschoolers are capable of controlling their world through social interactions and play. Such interaction with their peers enables preschoolers to achieve their goals to master the task of initiative and responsibility, which develops self-confidence. However, if a preschooler has overprotective parents, he or she may develop feelings of guilt.

Stage #4 Industry vs. Inferiority

Ages 6-12: Children begin comparing themselves to others. At this stage, they develop a sense of pride and accomplishment in all of their endeavors: academics, sports, social activities, and family. However, if children conclude that they don't measure up, then they develop an inferiority complex that can last until adulthood.

Stage #5 Identity vs. Role Confusion - YOLO Leader is Born

Ages 12-18: Erikson states that an adolescent's main task is developing a sense of self. This age group struggles with "Who am I?" and "What do I want to do with my life?" Adolescents experiment with different roles and ideas to see, which fits them best as they begin the journey to adulthood. Success at this stage provides them with a strong sense of identity to hold true to their beliefs. If they are confused at this stage, they will be confused as adults and struggle to "find" themselves.

Stage #6 Intimacy vs. Isolation

Ages 20-40: People who have developed a sense of self are ready to share life with others. Yet if people struggled with a sense of self earlier in life, they may have difficulty maintaining successful relationships and may experience loneliness and isolation.

Stage #7 Generativity vs. Stagnation

Ages 40 - 60 (Mid-life crisis): At this age, most people are concerned with generativity, which involves finding your life's work and contributing to the development of others such as volunteering, mentoring, or raising children. Men tend to buy a sports car, get tattoos, and take vitality supplements. Women, on the other hand, may be financially independent and are likely to file for divorce after years of marriage, concluding that the relationship hindered them from living out their dreams. Those who fail to master this task may experience stagnation and feel like they have nothing to offer to others, and are not concerned with productivity or self-improvement.

Stage #8 Integrity vs. Despair

Ages 60 - end of life: At this age, people either feel a sense of satisfaction or a sense of failure based on what they have or have not accomplished. Those who are proud of their accomplishments and feel a sense of integrity tend to look back over their life with few regrets. People on the other side of this personality may feel that their life was wasted and often self-talk about what they "would have," "should have," or "could have" been. Many exhibit feelings of bitterness, depression, and despair.

We've talked about Freud and Erikson's personality theories that both touch upon our early childhood environment. Another expert in this area is Jean Piaget. Piaget's cognitive development theory provides four stages of a child's mental development.[8] Piaget was the first psychologist to demonstrate the differences between how children think versus how adults think. He believed that children take an active role in their learning process, and they continuously build upon existing knowledge to adapt and add new information. According to Piaget, intelligence in children develops through a series of stages. These stages are:

- **Sensorimotor stage: birth to 2 years** - Children experience the world through reflexes, senses and motor responses;

- **Preoperational stage: ages 2 to 7** - Children learn a language and are egocentric and see things from their perspective;

- **Concrete operational stage: ages 7 to 11** - Children become more adept at using logic.

- **Formal operational stage: ages 12 and up** - Children develop an increase in logical reasoning and think hypothetically. They also grow in moral, ethical, social, and philosophical reasoning.

Finally, the fourth and final expert on personality and self-awareness is Lawrence Kohlberg's moral development theory. This is the one that I hang my hat on. What I like about Kohlberg is that his theory is based on the stages of moral reasoning, which are critical for YOLO leaders. Yet, he also touches on Piaget's cognitive development framework. Kohlberg's stages are:

Level 1

Stage 1: Ages birth - 2 - Preconventional (Obedience & Punishment)- This stage is seen in elementary-age children where they learn socially acceptable norms about behavior from an authority figure such as a parent or teacher.

During Level 1, this is the pre-morals stage, and the child does not understand or reason about moral issues nor has a concept of obligation to others or authority. Good is what feels good, and bad is what feels bad.

Level 2

Stage 3: Ages 4-10 - Conventional (Good boy/girl) - At this stage, children seek approval from others. They learn to abide by the law and respond to their role when given a task.

As the child moves into level 2, his responses to cultural norms are brought out by current circumstances. Moral judgments are made based on the anticipated reward or punishment, "I'll probably get this positive reward if I do this," or "I'll probably get this negative report if I do that." The child has no sense of a higher thinking morality that doesn't have an executable consequence right away. Therefore, a child may throw a ball and break a window and get grounded, which is an executable consequence that is experienced right away. However, throwing the ball and breaking the neighbor's window makes him feel bad doesn't even register on his radar because feeling bad doesn't affect him since they don't live in his house. Children at this stage also conform to group expectations.

Level 3

Stage 5: Ages 11- adult - Post-conventional (Social contract, principled conscience) - This is where we adopt a moral thinking pattern and consider the genuine interest of others.

At Level 3, this is where our morality sets in. Morality is defined in terms of a contract in avoiding violation of others' rights. We identify what is right and wrong and move into Stage 6, where we form our individual principles or consciousness at a higher level. It's our universal, ethical principle orientation, and rules do not guide us, but principles guide us— we know the speed limit is 55, and we do so because it is responsible. Being honest, kind, and responsible has been ingrained in me, so now I have developed it for myself.

All four of these renowned psychologists speak to how we develop our self-awareness. As you can see, they all agree that you develop your sense of awareness in your early childhood stage right around adolescence, where you realize there are rewards and punishments that you seek to receive or to avoid. In doing so, you develop self-awareness, and it is within *this* self that the YOLO leader can now establish his or her sense of how to lead. Chances are when most of us were in high school and college, and we were following the leader or the crowd as our self-autonomy had not been developed.

Just think about the endless possibilities if adolescents determine who they want to be at this early stage. Consider the leadership trajectories when peer pressure or cultural norms do not sway your children and grandchildren. Think about what society would look like if we get people to learn to lead themselves. Imagine everyone being driven by an internal moral compass that allows them to learn to lead at an early stage. With such a high level of character and moral thinking, we can increase our level of competency and productivity as a nation.

More importantly, encouraging young people to learn to lead themselves can increase the overall quality of our country. After all, it's easier to fix boys than to mend men. Likewise, it's easier to fix girls than to mend women. So before life gets in the way, learn to lead yourself and teach your children to do the same. Armed with a working knowledge of our cognitive development is a tool for becoming a YOLO leader.

"This above all: to thine own self be true..."
- William Shakespeare

CHAPTER 2

KNOW THYSELF

Self-awareness and self-control go hand-in-hand

We were first introduced to the term, "self-awareness," by psychologists Shelley Duval and Robert Wicklund in 1972. Duval and Wicklund view self-awareness as a primary mechanism of self-control. I agree and see it more of a marriage between the two terms because you cannot control something that you do not know exists. For example, if you don't believe you have an anger problem, then you won't do anything to correct it.

Similarly, if you don't acknowledge your weaknesses, you will continue living an unaware life, missing the opportunity for real growth. Chances are others around you see areas for improvement, but you are blind to your own self. The moment you become aware (have knowledge or perception of) and choose to address the problem, you are now on your way to the journey of having self-control.

Emotional Intelligence (EI) & (EQ)

Just as self-awareness and self-control work together, so does self-awareness and emotional intelligence. In his book, *Emotional Intelligence*, psychologist Daniel Goleman presents the theory that Emotional Intelligence (EI) or Emotional Quotient (EQ) is more valuable than a person's IQ.[9] Goleman defines self-awareness as "knowing one's internal states, preferences, resources, and intuitions."[10]

For those of us developing our self-awareness perceptions, Goleman defines EI or EQ as our ability to:

- * Recognize, understand, and manage our own emotions
- * Recognize, understand, and influence the emotions of others

In other words, we must be aware that our emotions drive our behavior, and those behaviors impact people (positively and negatively). Therefore, it is important to learn how to manage emotions, both our own and others, when under pressure.

We should also view self-awareness to include listening to our inner being to gain invaluable insight into our outer selves. We can become more self-aware by shifting our attention to specific details of our personality as well as our action or inaction to various events. Think about a recent emotional reaction of anger or outburst. What were the thought triggers? Is there a pattern? The great thing is that we all have the power to change our anger-driven interpretations. The more we engage in a deliberate, heightened awareness of our emotional responses to specific events, we will instinctively handle them better going forward—consistency is the key.

The amount of focus, time, and energy you invest in self-awareness will determine your level of success in life and leadership. Are you argumentative? Emotional? Easy going? Pensive? All of these personality behaviors have been shown to govern your leadership trajectory. Being self-aware allows you to control your reactions and emotions to situations that can change the outcome in your favor. It's not until you become fully aware of your thoughts, feelings, and actions that you can master your life's direction and draw more people to align with your vision.

Not only should individuals master emotional intelligence to build stronger relationships, but companies should also strive to grow in emotional intelligence. A great example can be seen in a 2019 story regarding Krispy Kreme Doughnuts and a Minnesota college student, Jayson Gonzalez. Jayson created a Facebook page, Krispy Kreme Run, Minnesota. After a feature story in the *St. Paul Pioneer Press* praising Jayson for his entrepreneurial spirit by driving 270 miles to the nearest Krispy Kreme in Iowa, the story went viral. Krispy Kreme's leadership ordered Jayson to stop delivering its doughnuts. Not long afterward, social media backlash ensued, and Krispy Kreme reversed course and allowed Jayson to become an independent operator for the brand and also provided him with 500 dozen doughnuts to resell. Leaders from various companies around the country praised Krispy Kreme for a valuable lesson learned in emotional intelligence.

Cultural Intelligence (CI) & (CQ)

Technology has made it incredibly easy to connect to the world by simply clicking a few buttons. It's as if the world is shrinking, and the word "global" is no longer some far off concept for Fortune 100 companies that we cannot grasp. Global applies to one-person operations and mid-sized businesses, as well. Now more than ever, leaders need to understand the cultural norms of individuals from other countries to cohesively and efficiently work together. Our society is becoming more and more diverse, so our knowledge and understanding of those who don't look like us, talk like us, dress like us, or function like us, must be in tune with our global constituents to build strong working relationships and be successful. YOLO leaders must be able to cross cultural boundaries to effectively communicate and solve critical problems in our own territory and places abroad. In her book, *Cultural Intelligence: The Competitive Edge for Leaders*,[11] Julia Middleton describes what it means for leaders to have cultural intelligence or a cultural quotient.

Middleton believes that good leaders need all three if they are going to lead effectively: IQ, EQ, and CQ. In all of these areas, we should be in a continuous learning mode to improve our understanding. Knowing your "Core" and

"Flex" and how they work will be advantageous in developing your CQ. Your "Core" consists of the things that are constant in your life—unmoveable, unchanging beliefs, and principles. "Flex" are those things that can be changed, and you are willing to be flexible in adapting to them. Balancing both your Core and Flex sets you on the right path towards increasing your CQ.

Once you begin to have a better understanding of who you are, then gaining knowledge and experiences from someone you trust is the next right step. To determine your CQ level, Middleton created an Eight Pole Assessment and questionnaire for you to send to your network for feedback to help fuel your journey. Middleton encourages you to connect with people who are different from you according to the following characteristics: generation, gender, faith, politics, perspective, disability, sector, and prospects. The Eight Poles[12] and links to her questionnaire are available in the Resources section.

Don't get frustrated if you cannot find a leader that you currently interact with in all of the poles. Middleton encourages you to start with one or two, and then the others will come along as you grow your CQ. A final point that she makes regarding CQ is the fact that millions of students receive the opportunity to study abroad yet hang out "with their own kind." This is truly a missed opportunity to develop a student's CQ, which can help further careers and build relationships. YOLO leaders should take advantage of every opportunity to engage with others who are different from them.

Take Action

Although focusing attention on our personality and other emotional attributes sounds easy, it can be difficult. I believe the primary reason is that "life" pushes and pulls us each day in many directions that cause distractions and a lack of observance of our behaviors. Most of the time, we are so set in the routine of how we handle situations that we don't know any other way to react. We become complacent in our minds and begin to self-talk and say things like, "this is who I am, take it or leave it." This type of attitude and dismissiveness will ultimately lead to dysfunction, stress, and discord in your environment. Consider the following activities below to help you become more self-aware.

YOLO Tips

1. Meditate or find some "alone time" for fifteen minutes each day. Studies show that there are several health benefits to practicing daily meditation, such as reducing stress and anxiety, improving emotional health, and enhancing self-awareness.

2. Journal your actions and thoughts each day. Make sure you write down your thoughts during significantly stressful times during your week.

3. Seek feedback from others to determine steps for improvement. Ask a spouse, sibling, or friend to rate you on a scale of 1-5, with "1" being less likely and "5" is most likely.

Question #1: Do I take personal responsibility for my actions?

Question #2: Am I the one who takes time to ask, "How are you?"

Question #3: Am I the one to speak up for others when they are wronged?

Question #4: Am I the one who takes the initiative to connect people to others?

*"An unexamined life is
not worth living."*
- Plato

CHAPTER 3

SELF-AWARENESS CHECKUP

There's no doubt that we must continue to grow and develop to understand who we are and what makes us tick. Every YOLO leader should start utilizing various self-awareness tools that will provide honest feedback. It is important to check in with your team members often to ensure that you are leading effectively and efficiently. Whether you use the Johari Window, The DiSC Personality Assessment, or 360 Degree Feedback, all can be great tools to keep you grounded and on course for self-improvement and future growth.

The Johari Window

During my graduate leadership studies at Cairn University, we worked extensively with the Johari Window Model to evaluate our self-awareness behaviors and personal development needs within our group. The model was derived by psychologists Joseph Luft and Harry Ingham in 1955, and the name, "Johari" is a combination of Joseph and Harry. The Johari Window is also known as the feedback and disclosure model of self-awareness.[13]

The model consists of four quadrants or "window panes," and the themes are based upon trust and feedback. If you share honest and revealing information about yourself to others, they will, in turn, provide honest feedback to help you learn about yourself in four critical viewpoints. When I think about this model, the story which comes to mind is the woman at the well in the Bible.[14] She went there knowing that no other women would be there—those who knew of her past. Yet she was surprised to meet Jesus, who knew everything about her and even things that she did not know about herself. We all have secrets and sides to us that we do not want to share, but if it is for the common good then we must find the courage to do so.

Window #1: Open/self-area or arena (What you see, and others see) – Consider your attitudes, behaviors, emotions, feelings, skills, and views that is known by you as well as by others.

Window #2: Blind self or blind spot (What others see but you don't see) – Information about you that others know, but you are unaware of and could be of benefit you in the long run.

Window #3: Hidden area or façade (What you see and others don't see) – Personal information about you that others do not know, such as fears, past experiences, and secrets.

Window #4: Unknown area (What no one sees)– Unknown information to you or others but is only revealed through communication, such as a traumatic experience or hidden capabilities.

Questions to examine:
1: What do you know about yourself that others don't know?
2. If they did know what impact would it have on them?
3. How do you think it impacts you?
4. Based on the above information, what lie have you been telling yourself?
5. How much energy or productivity has this lie cost you to keep up?

The Johari Window is a great tool to help you become more aware of who you are and how you show up at any given time. Place all of those things that you know about yourself within the quadrant and then invite others to provide a personal inventory. When working within the Johari model, it is important to realize that there is no right or wrong, good or bad, but it simply just "is."

One of the things about being a leader is that your followers know all of your weaknesses, no matter how hard you try to hide them, overlook them, or overcompensate. If the people following you know your flaws, and they genuinely love you, they will cover you. I'll end with a familiar story of Noah in the Bible. In Genesis Chapter 6, Noah built the Ark as God advised him to do. It was his job to tell the entire civilization at that time that it was going to rain. No one believed him since they had never seen rain before. Noah was obedient to God's command, built the Ark, and took the animals two by two of every male and female.

After the rain fell, Noah's family were the only survivors, and they took care of the land. They planted a vineyard, and Noah got drunk off the grapes and passed out. His three sons, Ham, Shem, and Japheth, were present. Ham looked upon his father's nakedness and exposed him, whereas Shem and Japheth got their father's cloak, held it up between them, and walked backward to cover him. When Noah awoke, he realized that his weakness was exposed, and he cursed Ham and his offspring. As a leader, you've got to have people around you that will cover you, not expose you.

Yes, those who expose you will let you down, but those let downs are going to happen, and they shouldn't devastate you. On a personal note, I remember when I was going through issues at my church. I had one of my leaders come to me and tell me several things that I was doing wrong as a leader. He mentioned that others stated that I wasn't taking criticism well, I wasn't talking to the people well, and several other things or expose your weakness. After he was finished, I thought to myself, *Man, if I was so bad, what were you doing to cover me? Did you ever speak up for me in those circles where I was being demonized?*

It all boils down to the fact that everybody needs to be self-aware. When you don't have someone fighting on your behalf or someone speaking well of you, then you have to learn to speak well of yourself. Leadership is not without criticism, nor is it without your vulnerabilities being exposed. I want to challenge you. Maybe you are a leader who needs to step out, but before you do, make sure that you really know yourself and this Johari Window is an excellent tool for you to know yourself and to get people you can trust to help you do this exercise regularly. Ask everyone connected to you: your spouse, co-workers, management team, and family. Who knows, the Johari Window may be the one thing to help you in your process of becoming the YOLO leader that you were designed to be.

DiSC® Personality Assessment: Dominance, Influence, Steadiness, Conscientious

The DiSC profile is a great non-judgmental tool to help determine your behavioral style. It is one of my favorite behavioral tools. Taking the DiSC® profile requires answering detailed questions on how you handle situations. As a certified DISC Trainer, I am familiar with all four types of people I will meet throughout my life. Each letter of the word "DiSC" describes the type of person and their characteristics. It's not like the Myers-Briggs test, which tells you "why you do what you do," whereas DiSC tells you what you commonly do in certain instances.

In the DiSC personality profile, most people want their profile to contain a high "D," Dominance. They think that having a high "D" is the one who gets most of the accolades and has the most fun. However, being a high "D" can drive people away. I am a high "I" Influence. I know that I can inspire people and motivate them. That's one of the reasons why I became a motivational speaker and also a life coach. Here's a very closely kept secret... I'm really an introvert at heart. When I'm at home, I like to sit and do nothing, but I've trained myself to show up for the moment. As a leader, you don't have to be a robot and act only one way with regard to your personality. This does not mean that you go against your integrity; it just means that you can show up when necessary.

Depending on the type of job you have, you can better understand the benefits of having different behavioral traits within your organization or team. For example, if you work at NASA and your role is to put people on the moon, you'd better have some conscientious people on your team that are astute with numbers and pay careful attention to detail. You want a team with people like Dorothy Johnson, as seen in the movie *Hidden Figures*. Ms. Johnson was in charge of not only making sure that the astronauts orbited the moon but made it back to land safely. Her numbers had to be exact. If she were a little off, the trajectory would have been wrong, and the possibility of reentering the Earth's orbit and landing in the ocean where the Navy could retrieve the pod would have been slim to none.

Consequently, if you work in a high sales environment like real estate or car sales, then you usually have high "I's" working in the field, and they're probably your best salespeople. Sales managers are likely your high "D's," but in the back office, you want to have "S" and "C's" for steadiness and conscientious. If you're the CEO of a corporation or the franchise player of a sports team, then you are likely a high "D." As you can see, each behavior trait has its benefits—there is no right and wrong personality trait.

For the longest, I was in denial of my personality profile. I really wanted to be a high "D." Over the years, I've learned that I am a high "I" for good reason because it is precisely what I do as a pastor, as a leader—inspire other people. It turns out, I'm right where I need to be, so don't begrudge where you are but embrace it in a sense that you can always work on sharpening your tools to becoming better. Once I learned to embrace who I was doors opened up a lot for me because I wasn't trying to walk in someone else's shoes anymore, especially when I first started pastoring.

You see, I thought pastors had to be a certain kind of way to attract people, so I made up my mind that I was going to be a "hooper" like the preachers in the Baptist Church who preached in a cadence that almost sounds like your singing with the organ as your background. I remember my wife telling me, "Jon, just be yourself." When I embraced my true self, I was comfortable, and I became more productive. Plus, all along, I was really a teacher, so I staff and surround myself with other traits that are different than mine. The YOLO leader knows where they fit, they know their skill set, and they know how to operate within their zone because they're going for flow. Once you get in your flow, you'll be fine.

360 Degree Feedback

Companies typically use 360 Degree Feedback to help you in your personal development growth plan. The process involves many people who you are connected to either as subordinates, peers, or upper management to complete a survey of questions about you in either an anonymous or identifiable manner. The survey questions are intended to measure your behaviors and competencies, how others perceive you, and skill sets such as communication, listening, goal-setting, character, and teamwork. Have you gone through this process at work? If so, have you improved upon areas that were highlighted as needing improvement?

For the feedback to be valuable, it has to be honest and truthful. There's been a push to move away from 360 feedback because those filling out the surveys were only providing positive messages for fear of hurting someone's feelings or embarrassment. So instead, research suggests that you should ask a person, "what or how could I have better handled a specific situation?" By asking for a recommendation on improvement, people are more apt to give honest, truthful feedback. Regardless of which self-awareness tool you choose, make sure to include those who genuinely want to see you grow.

"I count him braver who overcomes his desires than him who conquers his enemies; for the hardest victory is over self."
- Aristotle

CHAPTER 4

SELF-CONTROL

One of the things I've learned over the years is that there is freedom in the truth. Facing our realities, no matter how ugly, is the only way to overcome our personal struggles. We must get to a point where we stop lying to ourselves and embrace our limitations. I genuinely believe we can do all things through Christ, who strengthens us, but we have limitations and are often held back by our self-deception or even misunderstanding of what that means. The more we push ourselves beyond realistic limits, we hit a brick wall and give up, feeling like a failure. In reality, you have not failed, but you have been deceived by your own desires or expectations and have just experienced a truth—you can't do everything.

Self-control is the ability to master oneself from within. It means that you have to master and control your desires in every area of your life—what you eat, what you wear, what you do, and what you say. It affects your leadership abilities in your home, workplace, and relationships. Self-control requires maturity. It is a learning and growth process that does not happen overnight. As you mature, you begin to see that boundaries and limits are a good thing. Once you start to embrace your boundaries, moral, legal, physical, and spiritual, you will have a renewed sense of character and integrity to operate in various areas. In their book, *Boundaries*, Henry Cloud and John Townsend, talk about the need for boundaries and how embracing limitations is a good thing. Cars have speedometers for a reason. There are federal and state laws, rules, and regulations that limit our everyday life for a reason—although we may not agree with them, it is a societal way to have order and uniformity. Controlling our instincts to do or not do something is critical to our well-being, and more often than not, when we lose our self-control, we do so to our detriment. YOLO leaders recognize that, *although I can do something, it's best if I don't*. A primary function of YOLO leaders is that they must master self-control.

Relationships

Most of the time, when we hear of a leader's moral failure, it comes because they did not employ self-control. When celebrities like Harvey Weinstein, Bill Cosby, pastors, and others are called on the carpet for their sexual misconduct, it is a clear sign that they don't have self-control. The more you learn to master yourself from within, the happier and more successful your lives will be.[15]

How do you know when you need to exercise self-control? Here are a few scenarios:

* When you have a strong desire to do something pleasurable or in excess that you know is *not* the right thing to do;
* When you dread doing something, but you know it is good for you;
* When you need to remove the things from your life that you know are temptations; and
* When you learn how to manage stress because when you are stressed, you make poor decisions.

In his book, *Can't Hurt Me*, David Goggins tells the story of how he overcame an abusive father, low self-esteem, obesity, and working in a dead-end job. Despite his adversities, he became an elite combat soldier, Navy Seal, Army Ranger, and world-class endurance athlete. David learned to discipline his mind over his body. He redefined pain in his mind so that he could compete and achieve at the highest level.

Successful leaders understand they must master every single aspect of who they are and leave behind every excuse that hinders their personal growth and success. Again, self-control is about mastering oneself from within. It is about mastering yourself in the face of disappointments and mastering yourself in the face of setbacks. Mastering yourself when your reality is incongruent with our dreams. When you learn to master yourself, you will begin to create the world you've always wanted.

The Marshmallow Test

Let's face it; we all desire instant gratification. We live in a world where technology has set the tone for our lives to operate at warp speed. Today, we can have every necessity delivered to our doorstep within 24-hours. And if we cannot have it within that time frame, we are frustrated, stressed, and will more than likely take out our anger on an unsuspecting third party. Why have we become so impatient? Will one more day really make a difference in receiving a product that you don't need for another month? This all goes back to self-control and being able to master your emotions when a situation doesn't go according to your plans. How do you relax and shift gears until your package arrives?

In the 1960s, Stanford Psychologist Walter Mishel performed a test on young children demonstrating the significance of delayed gratification known as The Marshmallow Test. Children were given a marshmallow and promised another, only if they could wait 20 minutes before eating the first one. This test was an exercise in "delayed gratification." Years later, Mishel followed up with the participants and noticed that the children who waited 20 minutes to get the additional marshmallow experienced a more fulfilled and satisfying life. The ones who ate the marshmallow before the 20 minutes lapse, experienced a less than satisfied or fulfilled life.

While these results weren't conclusive and even criticized, the overall message was clear: delayed gratification brought greater success in life, while immediate or instant gratification brought satisfaction, the moment was fleeting and less fulfilling than waiting. How many times have you failed in the waiting game? Effective leaders have learned how to control their wants and desires. They understand the power of delayed gratification. Delaying gratification of the flesh is a sign of growth, discipline, and self-control.

How can we practice delayed gratification?
From a financial perspective, when the housing boom hit the U.S. in the '90s, everyone was buying houses that they could not afford. One T.V. station highlighted a Florida exotic dancer who was in the process of buying three houses simultaneously. Once the bubble burst in 2008, many people lost a lot of money, including financial expert, Dave Ramsey. In his book, *The Total Money Makeover*, Ramsey tells how he had to file bankruptcy because he invested beyond his financial ability. His desire for money clouded his mind. I, too, have gotten caught up in the housing bomb. Fortunately, I stepped back and realized that I needed to slow down. Albert Einstein said, "the 8th Wonder of the World is compound interest;" it's slow, it's not exciting, it's not in your face, but when you learn to wait, it is the most wonderfully fantastic thing in the world.

There are significant benefits to slowing down. Namely, you get to exercise muscles that you usually do not use. These include patience, humility, and the "wait" muscle. Most of us are kinesthetic learners—we learn by doing. For me, kinesthetic learning is helpful, and I am more confident once I have hands-on experience doing something. As a YOLO leader, experience is the best teacher.

Lies & Coverup

"A lie can travel halfway around the world,
While the truth is putting on its shoes."
*– **Charles Spurgeon***

People lie for various reasons. We all have done it. Sometimes we lie to save ourselves from embarrassment, to protect someone, to avoid the consequences of our actions, or just for the sheer thrill of it. Lying is seductive. It's sexy, tantalizing, enticing, and it feels good—that's why we do it. One of the biggest challenges with a lie is that one lie is never enough, and they quickly turn into the snowball effect. You have to cover one lie with another lie and another until it is out of control, and the lie is exposed, causing a considerable amount of damage.

It's even more alarming when companies lie to consumers and place profits over lives. The pharmaceutical industry is notorious for not disclosing all of the data on the effects and other critical information to using its drug. It appears that big lies and big money go together, and the risk of lawsuits and payouts are incidental to doing business. In 2015, news spread that Volkswagen fitted over 600,000 diesel cars with software to circumvent U.S. emission tests. The software switched on emission controls during tests and automatically shut off during regular driving. The Volkswagen cover-up stemmed from the top down, and Volkswagen has agreed to pay billions in compensation to U.S. purchasers. Why would the CEO of a multibillion-dollar company risk his position and consumer trust with a lie?

Like the Volkswagen lies and cover-up, there was the Theranos cover-up by a young woman hailed as the female Steve Jobs. Her name is Elizabeth Holmes, and her story of founding a revolutionary billion-dollar blood-testing company made headlines, a bestselling book, and a TV movie. The problem was that Holmes' lies were exposed, and she was ousted as the CEO and charged with massive fraud. She claimed that she created a microfluidic chamber that could run several different blood tests from one drop of blood. Holmes began doing damage control by lying and covering up results for at least two years. The SEC found that Holmes defrauded investors and potential customers even though Theranos had a market value of $9 billion.

More recently, in October 2018, we witnessed a tragic crash of the Boeing Max Jet 737, Flight 610 from Jakarta, Indonesia, that crashed minutes after takeoff killing 189 people. A few months later, in March 2019, Ethiopian Airlines Flight 302 crashed after takeoff killing 157 people on board. As a result of the second crash, all Boeing Max flights were grounded in the U.S. and around the globe. Black box data and other evidence concluded that there was a malfunction in an automated alert system that pilots were unaware of until the crash.[16] Also, a Boeing senior engineer stated that Boeing rejected a safety system to keep costs down, which could have reduced the risks of the deadly crashes. There was additional evidence that a chief technical pilot believed the Max had "egregious" issues. In the end, Boeing put dollars over human lives, and their cover-up is out in the open. Boeing is involved in ongoing investigations for violations by the National Transportation Safety Board, The Justice Department, and the FBI as part of a criminal investigation. Hopefully, other companies will take heed to the downfall and public mistrust of Boeing and other highly-valued stock companies by using better moral judgment in the future.

Make the Right Choice

"He who prides himself with wealth
and honor hastens his own downfall."
- Lao Tzu

Each one of us has our own definition of success. When we work so hard on that "thing," which we are most passionate about and it takes off, there is no greater feeling. Success and hard work go hand in hand. However, instant success can shift our focus, drive, and emotions. When fame or notoriety happens overnight, it doesn't afford us the time to connect with our inner feelings and prepare ourselves in the event of a fall. Often, we need to step back and reevaluate our quick rise and fall from another viewpoint. Regardless, we need to take a deep breath, relax, and hold ourselves accountable for our fall. Sometimes a good public exposure and shame can be beneficial. When you go through a personal downfall in public, two things happen 1) you realize the shame, and it takes you to a place of repentance; or 2) you realize the shame and take on a worldly sorrow position which will lead to downfall. The choice is yours: Godly sorrow leads to repentance, and a chance to start over, worldly sorrow leads to your demise.

The Bible tells us of two men, David, and Judas and how both of them dealt with shame and sorrow. This difference is pointed out in Scripture after David had an affair with Bathsheba, he had her husband Uriah killed. David had Godly sorrow,[17] whereas Judas had worldly sorrow. David repented for his sins and went on to become a great King. Judas, on the other hand, betrayed Jesus for "thirty pieces of silver" and realized the gravity of what he had done and hung himself — facing the music when you get caught forces you to choose your future. Unfortunately, many people in positions of trust and authority choose the worldly sorrow solution, such as Philip Baker, an Assistant Principal in Texas convicted of engaging in child pornography committed suicide in prison. [18] More recently, a pastor and decorated detective in Florida committed suicide after the FBI found child pornography on his computer.[19] Again, when we get caught lying or committing heinous acts against another person, we need to make the right decision. First, tell the truth, repent, and face the consequences, good or bad. If we lie to avoid taking responsibility for our actions, that lie will ultimately catch up to us, causing additional harm. YOLO leaders strive to make the right choice after a fall.

The Dreaded Asterisk

You don't want to be a leader with an asterisk beside your name. That is, you do great things, yet there's an unflattering footnote connected to your name. Household names have been tarnished forever like Barry Bonds: steroid scandal, Martha Stewart: insider trading, and Lance Armstrong: long-time doping and cheating. The urge to cheat in some form or fashion is present, whether your occupation is a professional athlete, celebrity, pastor, business owner, or employee. We have to fight for this thing. The urge to give in to your base self is always there. It is a constant fight. It can make or break you. Self-control is powerful. I was at an event, and I started talking to a guy I met in an earlier session. As we were walking along the corridor, he said, "I only read biographies of dead people because I know how they end." Every leader who is alive is writing his or her story as we speak, make sure yours has a happy ending.

In Jim Collins' book, *How the Mighty Fall: And Why Some Companies Never Give In*, Collins outlines the five stages of decline.[20]

Stage 1: Hubris Born of Success: The more success you have, the more likely you are to make poor decisions. Success can isolate people from the real world. Arrogance kicks in, and you become unteachable and unreachable. Leaders begin to believe their own headlines.

Stage 2: Undisciplined Pursuit of More: Since Stage 1 made you feel like you could do anything, in this stage, you *try* to do everything. You no longer rely on sound judgment, and you begin to focus on "I want this." You overestimate who you are and what you can do. Integrity is no longer your goal—expediency or bust!

Stage 3: Denial of Risk and Peril: Leaders avoid the clear and present risks and move ahead in spite of the warning signs. Romanticism replaces reality. People around you avoid telling you the truth and tell you what you want to hear. Huge, unwise, and imprudent decisions are made, yet you don't take personal responsibility for failure. It's always someone else's fault.

Stage 4: Grasping for Solutions: At this stage, leaders are looking for a "savior," whether a person, program, or product. This is where leaders will throw a proverbial "Hail Mary" to see what they can do to save themselves.

Stage 5: Capitulation to Irrelevance or Death: Alas, as a leader, you finally admit defeat. All options are spent, and winning is not on the horizon.

All of these stages of decline are avoidable if leaders learned to practice humility and self-control. It is essential to focus on success but also to study failure and learn what *not* to do. Always remember that success does not always happen in a straight line.

Failure Perspective

"Remember that failure is an event, not a person."
- Zig Ziglar

All too often, when things don't turn out as we expected, we take the negative outcome extremely personal and describe ourselves as being a failure. We convince ourselves that we're not good enough to garner success in whatever area we're trying to grow. Instead of beating ourselves up, we should take an honest and introspective look at our role in the situation and see if there is a learning experience or areas for improvement. Consider these mindset shifts:

1. <u>Remember that things will not always be the way they are right now</u>. If you're doing good now, just wait. If you aren't doing good now, just wait. Learn to identify and appreciate your current season.

2. <u>Remember that you can always learn something</u>. No one has cornered the market on knowledge, and they never will. So always read books, watch videos, attend learning workshops—find ways to be a continuous learner.

3. <u>Get rid of pride</u>. Pride is always a precursor to failure. If you don't know if you are prideful, ask a spouse, family member, friend, or coworker—they will tell you the truth.

4. <u>Change before you have to</u>. Change is inevitable, so you must embrace the changes in your life. If you change because you have no alternative, then you will be less in control and more resistant.

5. <u>Seek cheap experiences</u>. The best way to get cheap experiences is by getting a mentor, talking to a counselor, or seeking the advice of a wise sage to learn from your mistakes. Costly experience is the experience you pay for yourself.

Stay the course. Don't allow hubris to set in. In all transparency, I had to pray for this chapter on self-control because I could fall in this place as well. I don't want to come across as a person who has made it or has arrived. I am striving to become a YOLO leader, as well.

Fundamental Principles from YOLO Leaders on Mastering Self Control

Principle #1: When you fail to practice self-control, you will be impulsive in your actions, unrestrained in your impulses, and careless with your emotions.

Principle #2: When you fail to practice self-control, you will lose the things that are rightfully yours.

Principle #3: You can never gain through sacrifice what was lost through disobedience.

Principle #4: Practicing self-control is the hardest thing in the world to do.

Principle #5: It takes time to master yourself. It can take days, weeks, months, years, and even decades to learn how to master yourself.

Principle #6: The result of mastering self-control is always a greater reward than the thing you lost or had to give up.

YOLO Exercises:

#1. Write down three areas in which you wished you had implemented self-control.

#2. Identify factors that you believe resulted in your unsuccessful outcome.

#3. Develop a plan or strategy on how you will demonstrate self-control or delayed gratification. (When you have a plan in place, you are more likely to succeed the next time you are faced with the option of diving in instead of waiting.)

#4. Name three other people you will commit to helping develop self-control in their lives.

#5. Forgive yourself for the failures of your past.

"The weak can never forgive.
Forgiveness is the attribute
of the strong."
- Mahatma Gandhi

CHAPTER 5

FORGIVE & MOVE FORWARD

I like to think of forgiveness as a tool—it is critical to growth. Learning how to forgive is an essential aspect of our life because you are going to meet people who rub you the wrong way. Some people will take advantage of you, steal from you, and even lie on you because they more than likely are going through challenges. They haven't yet realized that they need to be a YOLO leader. However, since you are on a path to becoming a YOLO Leader, you understand that forgiveness will give you the necessary peace to move forward in your life. It may also provide you with room to feel compassion and empathy for the person who wronged you. There is a Biblical principle to forgiveness as the Lord's Prayer tells us to forgive us of our trespasses as we forgive those who trespass against us.[21] Jesus moved with compassion, and something supernatural took place. If a person truly moves in forgiveness, he will be forgiven. America loves when a person looks straight into the camera and asks for forgiveness.

It's been said that forgiveness is like a key to a prison cell; once you forgive someone, you take the key that you've been holding the whole time, and you let yourself out of prison. All too often, when it comes to forgiving others, many of us wait for the other person to make a move to show some signs that they had abused us or taken advantage of us. We're waiting for them to acknowledge that they've wronged us, and once they acknowledge us, then we will forgive them. Yet YOLO leaders must forgive first and unlock our minds from the prison of our past. Don't stay stuck in the moment. Many people are stuck in life because they're waiting for someone to forgive them. Are you waiting for your boss to acknowledge that he overlooked you for a promotion? Are you waiting for your spouse to admit that he or she doesn't appreciate you? How many of you are waiting for your children to say "thank you for everything," and "we love you."

In rare cases, the person(s) that offended us makes the first move and apologizes and asks for forgiveness. However, for the majority of us, we never receive the apology, or that person was unaware that they offended us, so the miscommunication and hurt feelings linger. The word "forgive" has an interesting meaning "for" and "give." All of us can give something, which means that you have something to offer.

You can't give something that you don't have. So the word "forgiveness" starts with the premise that you have something that you're holding on to. If you were hurt in dealing with that person, then you need to take that hurt and give it back to the person. Yes, we literally give it back to them.

I can't help but think about the times when my wife brings me something, and she wants me to put my hand out to receive it. I might say, "you can put it down over there." She gets frustrated when she gives me something, and I don't accept it at that moment. So when you don't extend your hand and receive something handed to you, the best thing to do is walk away because now you've given them back what they gave you. Who knows, they may not even realize what they gave you, but you're going to bring it back and leave it out in the open.

Who is it that you need to forgive? Stop right now and put this book down. Don't read another section until you first go back and forgive that person. Maybe it was a professor in college, a co-worker, a teammate, a mentor, or even a mentee that you trained. Did they steal your idea or fail to give you credit? Forgiveness is for you, not the person who wronged you. Always keep in mind that you are forgiving them for your well-being—not theirs. You don't want to bring the past into your future. It is so freeing to move into the future with no hindrances or baggage.

In the book, *The Art of War* by Sun Tzu talks about the first-mover advantage in that whoever is first in the field and awaits the coming of the enemy will be fresh for the fight.

Whoever is second in the field and has to hasten to battle will arrive exhausted. So go ahead and forgive people now so that you can be vibrant and fresh for the battle of life to win.

I think one of the most powerful exercises of forgiveness occurred when I was working with our youth and several other youth and leaders in Philadelphia at a weekend event. Many of the young boys were dealing with hurt and pain from past absent or neglectful parents. Many of the young women were also dealing with the same issues as well.

In this group, we did a simple exercise and had each teen sit in a chair, and we had another chair facing them. The person in the chair facing them was a representation of the person who had hurt them, and they were going to release the hurt, anger, and resentment to move forward. I remember sitting down in the chair, and a 16-year-old girl sat across from me. Her father had not been in her life, and she longed to have his affection. As she looked me in the eye, she said, "Daddy, I forgive you I hold nothing against you." We asked the teens to repeat their words of forgiveness three times. By the third time, the room of the atmosphere shifted, tears flowed, and her voice trembled, "Daddy, I forgive you, and I hold nothing against you." There was silence in the room. We all saw something break for that young lady that was the most powerful experience that she's ever had in her life. I want you to have that same experience and prepare to say it to whoever that person is that caused you pain. I guarantee that if you repeat it enough times and mean it from the heart, then you'll begin to enter into the next phase of your life with nothing hindering you.

Finally, studies have shown that there are adverse health consequences of not forgiving a person. Many people operating in unforgiveness walk around with emotional baggage of pain, anger, hate, bitterness, and resentment. Don't be a person who misses out on the liberation of forgiveness. Make the right choice, forgive, and be free!

"For as he thinketh in his heart, so is he..."[22]
- Proverbs 23:7

CHAPTER 6

THE HOLY GAILs

No, it's not a typo. GAIL is an acronym that is used to describe our thought process that, in essence, becomes energy blockers and defaults to our awareness. **GAILs** stand for **G**remlins, **A**ssumptions, **I**nterpretations, and **L**imiting Beliefs. We all have them, and we give them so much weight and ultimately allow them to hold us back in our lives. Your **Gremlins** are the internal voices that tell you you're not good enough, and it causes you to doubt everything about yourself. **Assumptions** are based on your past experience, and if something happened before, you assume it will occur again. In fact, in a study, people were asked to write down their worries over a period of time and then write what actually happened. Would you believe that 85% of what people worried about never happened? More important, of the 15% where a worry did come to fruition, 79% were able to handle it without the stress and devastation they initially feared. Technically, this means that 97% of what we worry about keeps us locked in fear.[23]

The **Interpretations** in GAILs is your opinion of a situation or event that you hold true, whether it's actually true or not. Finally, an Interpretation are all of those self-limiting things that you accept about life, others, or your circumstances that stifle your way of growing and thinking. One example of Limiting beliefs happened to me on the phone with a family friend that I had known for over ten years. As she was talking, I dropped the phone. I was startled by a spider and instinctively went to kill it. When I picked up the phone, she had hung up. A few days later, she said to me, "Jonathan, if I offended you, I'm sorry. I think it was something I said that made you drop the phone and not come back." I was thinking, *What*? I replied, "Oh no, I had to kill a spider!"

Unfortunately, we are naturally prone to think negatively, and we have to be taught to think more positively. It's like the guy who was invited to the football game. Each time the team huddled, he was nervous because he believed they were talking about him. Our problem is that we have to make meaning of things regardless of their validity. Since we are innately "meaning" people, we should interpret more events as positive. I have been in small groups where men share that no one in their family went to college or had successful marriages; therefore, they believe that a similar fate will happen to them. We have to rewrite our own script and change the narrative. Limiting beliefs trap you and keep you going in circles. We all have the ability to reprogram our minds and shift our perspective.

Trust me, I know it's easier said than done, but you have to get to the point in your self-awareness where you acknowledge your thoughts, feelings, and behaviors so that instead of feeding and empowering your GAILs, you can shut them down in an instant. The more conscious you are of the process, the more power you will have to defeat the nagging, negative voices. My goal is for you to feel like you can own and have control of your life and put those GAILs to rest.

I was in a training class when my "Ah-ha" moment surfaced to eliminate my Gremlin. The trainers taught us to reprogram our brain with positive self-talk and refute the Gremlin's engagement. My Gremlin was, "Jonathan, you are just not good enough." This tape had played over and over in my head for too long. Yet the ironic thing about my Gremlin is that up to that point, I had done significant things in my life personally and professionally, and somehow that Gremlin was still there. I believe that we are all good enough to do any and everything that God called us to do. Now, it was my turn to face the things that I desired, which I believed were out of my league, with boldness and courage. Now and then I think to myself, *I wish I heard about this 20 years ago! I have been frustrated for so long.* There is no magic pill to get this right in your head, yet you have to put in some work on the inside. Continue to feed your spirit positively on the inside. Once you tap into the inside and set it straight, the outside will be an appealing reflection on the inside.

As a Christian, one of the most powerful tools I have at my disposal is Scripture. Regardless of your belief system, there is something significant that happens when you begin to believe truths about yourselves. To get your thoughts right, you have to first bombard your mind with words of life and not death. Words that build up and not tear down. These "anabolic" or "building up" statements below will do just that—build you up.

YOLO Tips

Practice these affirmations daily. You have to own it and speak it with intentionality to begin the process of quieting your Gremlin:

1. *" I am fearfully and wonderfully made. I am an original, and my contributions are necessary and needed in the lives of others."*

2. *" I am here on purpose, and I am accepted and loved by God for a purpose."*

3. *" My true worth and value are not reflected in the job I have, the house I live in, our the car I drive. But rather, it is determined by the One who created me."*

4. *"Today, whatever I put my hands on will prosper and be successful."*

5. *"I am a problem-solver, and people seek me out and pay me handsomely because I get results."*

Part II

YOLO
Apprenticeship

"Inaction breeds doubt and fear. Action breeds confidence and courage. If you want to conquer fear, do not sit home and think about it. Go out and get busy."
- Dale Carnegie

CHAPTER 7

QUIT WASTING TIME

If you are waiting for life to start, then you are already too late. If you don't like the direction your life is going, then you have to take control of it. Time is a precious commodity, and we must use it wisely. No matter what grand plans you make in your New Year's resolutions, there will never be a perfect time for you to make changes in your life to become a YOLO leader. Life will always get in the way, so the best thing that we can all do is to take a bold step towards change *today*. Whether you go through a self-awareness exercise, research personal leadership development strategies, or embark upon a continuous learning journey that includes emotional and cultural intelligence, there is no time like the present. What's holding you back from becoming better?

Envision the future and implement a plan action by **(i)**
Taking control: You have more control over your life than
you may believe. Although you cannot predict the future, as
the main character in your life story, begin to chart a positive
path and always strive for growth; **(ii) Writing the vision**:
What is your vision for your life? Write the vision and make it
plain.[24] Don't let others dictate your future. Begin writing out
your strategy in clear, specific terms. Who do you want to be?
What steps do you need to take to get there? What milestones
are important? How will you define success? Have a plan to
accomplish at least two goals each day; **(iii) Integrating your
vision**: Visions and dreams are great, however, implement-
ing them into your daily life is the only way to achieve more
significant outcomes. Be consistent in exhibiting positive attitudes and behaviors in your actions and all of your relationships. Integration is intentional, so be intentional about your
mindset shift to change, grow, and become a YOLO leader.

Time-Savers

YOLO Leaders understand that time is money. You can't
create time, nor rob time—it's a fixed commodity. If you
want to stop wasting money, start managing your time
better. If you manage it effectively, you can actually gain
more. On lifehack.org, they list the top 20 time-wasters
and the top five worthwhile activities you can do instead.
I'll share a few of the time-wasters that resonated with me.
According to the list, the number one time-waster is Facebook. Unless you're using the site to build your contact list

or networking, you are wasting time spending hours upon hours browsing your feed. They recommend consolidating your social media by using sites like Hootsuite or Zoho to organize all of your social media activities. So if you're posting pictures, you can send one photo to three or four different sites at one time.

Another big time-waster is personal grooming. Yes, of course, you need to take care of your appearance, but you shouldn't spend hours grooming yourself each day. Instead, develop a routine where you have all of your hair care and other grooming products in order. You should have your clothing pressed the night before. For all of the YOLO Leaders, you need to have a simplified wardrobe with a few mix and match items. Maybe two or three suits, that are always clean and pressed. Have your shirts laundered and ironed. Invest in quality apparel as they will last longer. Also invest in quality, comfortable shoes.

You can also save time by being faithful to your spouse or partner. Stay committed to your relationship, and don't spend so much time and money sneaking around with someone else. You should also limit your T.V. time. T.V. is a waste of time as 99% of what you're watching is not useful unless you're using it to build a skill or enhance some knowledge you already have. Most people don't realize that a regular 28-minute program has more than 18 minutes of commercials, and those commercials are there to convince you to spend more money. Consider investing in streaming services such as Netflix, Apple TV+, Hulu, Amazon Fire TV, or Disney+, for example. In this way, you determine when you want to watch a program or receive information about a particular subject.

Shopping is another time-waster. Most of you hate to go shopping, but you end up spending hours going from one store to the next. I would encourage you to shop online. For example, if you see an item in the store, make a note of it, or if there is a designer that you like, try to find the styles online. Be sure to take accurate measurements of yourself. Once you find a designer that fits you well, you will know your size in that line of clothing. Another YOLO tip for online clothing shopping: buy several pieces in bulk when they are on sale or the end of the season. You may also get better deals for specific shopping days like Black Friday, Memorial Day, or Labor Day. Buying in bulk has the advantages of saving time and money, but it also means that you may have to get rid of a lot of your stuff to make room for your new things. However, organizing clothes is another time-waster.

The final time-waster I want to mention is setting up solo meetings. These are meetings where there is only one purpose. Since you are going to have a meal during work hours, have a breakfast or lunch meeting. If you exercise or play golf during the day, invite that person to come along if it is also an activity that they do, and have an informal meeting. You must maximize your time each day and do more than one thing in your session. Another thing you can do to stay organized and utilize time wisely is to use your mobile device as your personal assistant. You can speak into your device, and it will schedule your day and help you keep track of things. Also, if you're a manager or if you are involved in training, you can automate a lot of your recurring training events, so you do not have to be present for each one. For example, if you're a pastor and you have a new member orientation or if you're a superintendent of a school and have static teacher training, you can use your mobile phone to record your sessions or have your AV department assist you. This provides consistency of your policies and procedures. All of the videos can be maintained on a secure site with a personal login to view. All of these time-savers are simple practices to implement in your life that will help you manage your time more effectively.

Who's in Your Ear?

"Without consultation and wise advice, plans are frustrated, but with many counselors, they are established and succeed."
- Proverbs 15:22 (AMP)

To go farther in achieving your vision, you will need the help of other people. The possibilities are endless when two or more people come together with a common goal. When two or three are gathered in my name, I am with them.[25] Connect with others who are of a like-minded spirit to move your vision to the next level. There are advantages to working with others to accomplish something bigger than yourself. First, having different perspectives gives you a bigger picture of your initial plan and sparks innovation. Second, you are likely to be inspired by another viewpoint. Third, you have the support of others, and you also have accountability partners to encourage you to do your part and get things done.

So if you want to be your best, make sure you surround yourself with the best people. However, there will be those who will bring negative, toxic energy into your environment. Don't waste time accommodating or entertaining any negativity. If something or someone is weighing you down, you must rid yourself of the burden to soar. Scripture tells us to lay aside every weight and sin that entangles us so that we can run with persistence and perseverance.[26] This race in life requires us to be diligent and determined. Stay the course.

Avoid Negative Energy

Negative people are all around us. As a YOLO Leader, you have to decide what type of person you are going to be. Are you going to be a positive person or a negative person? Positivity and negativity is a choice. You can decide to shift your perspective to a more optimistic outlook and see things the way they could be as opposed to how they are. As a YOLO Leader, you should see yourself as a solution to solving problems. You have the power to create your future.

Do you know people who always see the glass as half empty? Are you the person who sees the glass as half full? Another way to look at positive and negative people is to say; there are trainable people and drainable people. When I worked in corporate America, there was a woman in the office who was the most negative person I've ever met—she never had a good thing to say. We were in customer service, so our job was to work with customers to make their payments. Her negativity overtook her entire personality. Even when she wanted to experience something good, she couldn't because her negativity kept canceling it out. She ended up leaving our company. I was so happy because when she left, the attitude in the organization changed. Negative people can bring down your whole organization.

You have to decide who's going to be in your organization or your circle because either people are going to build your life up by exhibiting anabolic energy qualities, or they're going to tear your life down by showing catabolic energy qualities. Energy leadership characteristics are discussed in the next chapter. How do you move from being a negative person to a positive person? The first thing you have to do is change your mind by filling it with positive affirmations and a positive attitude. I attended Dr. Alex Ellis' national Speak Up Conference, and he emphasized that you have to develop a winning mindset and speak positive daily affirmations into your life. Keep them in a place where you will see them each day. You can write out messages like "I have value, I am in control of my day, I will have a positive day, and I will make things happen." You have to start saying these things because there's power in your words.

The next thing you can do is find a group where people are doing more than you in an area where you have a similar interest. This type of group will challenge you to grow and step up. If you're the smartest one in your group, then you have to find a new group. Another thing you can do is invest in yourself. What books are you reading? What podcasts are you listening to? What Ted Talks are you watching? Make a conscious decision to change something in your routine. Listen to motivational or inspirational audiobooks while you're doing something else.

A final step that you can take to change from negative to positive is to watch what you eat. Diet and exercise is an essential part of your well-being. Cut out the junk food and fatty foods. A rule of thumb is that if it takes a short amount of time to cook or if you can pay to order it in a drive-thru, then you probably don't need to have it often. I love Chick-fil-A's number one meal, but I know I can't have it all the time. I switch it up and get a salad from Costco or BJs. There's nothing better than preparing your meals at home and eating fresh foods; food that's alive will give you life. Eating a healthy diet, along with exercise, will affect your mindset. Changing your attitude and perspective is within your reach as you are becoming a YOLO Leader.

Comparison Game

*"Stay in your lane. Comparison
kills creativity and joy."*
- Brené Brown

Comparing yourself to others is the biggest distraction to your YOLO transformation. Of course, there's nothing wrong with being inspired by what other successful people are doing. Still, if you always compare yourself to the next person, and it makes you feel inferior, then you need to reprogram your mindset and focus on competing with the most important person: yourself.

More often than not, a person's outward appearance has no bearing on their internal struggles. We all have external differences, but no one can compare to you internally. The outer is superficial and does not last. Now more than ever, social media has created a "look at me" syndrome where everyone is posting images of their lavish vacations, cars, homes, you name it. Some photos may be real, and others are fake, yet something inside us makes us feel inferior and wish that we had all of the trappings of success like those in our news feed. Studies have shown that there is a correlation between depression, anxiety, and low self-esteem in young adults who use social media platforms regularly.[27] We've already seen how social media can be a major culprit in time-wasting. Find positive and motivating activities to make you feel good about yourself and your life's journey.

It Starts With a Lead

What is it that you really want to accomplish? Narrowing down your focus will get you to the finish line a lot sooner. In *The Four Disciplines of Execution: Achieving Your Wildly Important Goals* (WIGS), by Chris McChesney, he lays out four key steps to achieve your WIGS. Step One requires you to focus on your WIG. Zero in on what must be done and how you intend to do it, you will be on your way to completion. This first WIG is so vital that if you don't do it, your entire plan will not work. Step Two is to act on the 80/20 "Lead" measures. McChesney states that twenty percent of your activities should lead to eighty percent of results. When you focus on the lead measures, you can predict the "lag" measures.[28] Lead is what are you doing upfront versus lag, which are the outcomes you get in the end. One of the best examples to understand this process can be seen in setting weight loss goals. If you want to lose 10 pounds, which is a lag measure, you must eat healthy, walk 30 minutes a day, and exercise, which are lead measures. I like the lead and lag principles because I believe if you apply these same principles to your life at different stages, no matter where you are and build upon them, you will achieve your wildest goals and find fulfillment. Here are a few lead measures to consider:

- I'm going to read more books
- I'm going to connect with more people
- I'm going to be present with my family
- I'm going to take risks at my job
- I'm going to eat healthy
- I'm going to join a gym

Whatever that stage is, you need to start now and just quit wasting precious time.

"Anabolic energy is the good stuff that needs to rise to the top in all of us to become exceptional YOLO leaders."

CHAPTER 8

ENERGY LEADERSHIP

Now that you've learned a great deal about yourself through honest self-evaluation, what are you going to do with this information? How will you overcome those issues or weaknesses moving forward? The truth about yourself is hard to face. The only thing to replace a lie is a powerful truth. Find one fact that you are willing to acknowledge and share. This is a great place to begin and gain the necessary energy to become an effective YOLO leader.

Do you often overreact to challenging situations at home or work and have to apologize later? Are you giving off positive or negative energy? We all have different energy levels that guide how we interact with others. Bruce Schneider defines our energy levels in his book, *Energy Leadership,*[29] in terms of anabolic and catabolic energy. For years I was only familiar with the word "anabolic" as it related to steroid use in athletes. All of the negativity surrounding the issue gave me the impression that anything "anabolic" was bad. However, anabolic energy is the constructive, building, and healing energy. It is that testosterone release that makes you feel good. Catabolic, on the other hand, is draining, destructive energy. Which side of the fence do you want to be on? As a YOLO leader, your focus should be on becoming a great anabolic leader first to yourself and then to others. There is truth in anabolic energy, and it can create a better world around you. If you are living your authentic self, you can start building upon your anabolic energy right now.

Studies show that 85% of leaders in the world are operating in a catabolic energy state.[30]

On the flip side, stress is likely the culprit for those of us functioning in a catabolic energy state. When this happens, cortisol is produced in the adrenal glands to help you control stress, but if you are always in stress overload, then high cortisol levels can lead to serious health issues. When you are stressed, anger and outbursts are visible displays of your attempt to cope with a situation. Chances are, if you are angry, anxious, and worried all the time, those around you are exhibiting the same negative energy. We all have seven levels of energy guiding our daily thoughts: 1) Victim, 2) Conflict,

3) Responsibility, 4) Concern, 5) Reconciliation, 6) Synthesis, and 7) Non-Judgmental.[31]

For those operating in Level 1, with a victim mentality, they tend to be apathetic and don't care about anything except how they are feeling. Level 2 individuals exert conflict-type energy, usually operating in anger, yet they get things done at all costs. Level 3, energy of responsibility, is those with a constant desire to cooperate with others and see both sides of a situation. Level 4 people are operating at Level with concern and compassion for others and have a servant attitude. Reconciliation at Level 5 is the person who gives off good vibes. They are peacekeepers and find ways to include everyone in the process. People with Level 6, synthesis energy, are happy and usually encouraging others with their knowledge and wisdom. Finally, Level 7 people are passionate about what they do and are creators. Which energy level do you flow in most? If you are operating at a low energy level, what can you do to move to more favorable levels?

When YOLO leaders understand the power of their leadership style and energy level, they can vacillate between their energy levels and capacity as appropriate. For example, you can become a situational leader and rise to the occasion like Dr. Martin Luther King Jr. Initially, King did not want to become a leader for equality, but when he heard about bus boycotts in Alabama, he knew he had to be there. He was a man who rose to the occasion. I don't think there is such a thing as a born leader. Instead, like King, some leaders rise to the occasion. Therefore, we have to know and be confident in the type of leader we are so that we can build and strengthen ourselves to handle the uncertainties ahead. People will follow leaders who are cool, calm and collected when faced with challenges. Your followers will feed off of your vibe, and chances are they will be happy, relaxed, and more engaged in your vision.

Anabolic energy is the good stuff that needs to rise to the top in all of us to become exceptional YOLO leaders. There are eight principles that all YOLO leaders need to master along their anabolic energy leadership journey: A=Authentic, N= Nice, A= Accurate, B= Brilliant, O= Open-minded and Objective, I= Integrated, and C= Character.

"One positive word can change a negative situation."

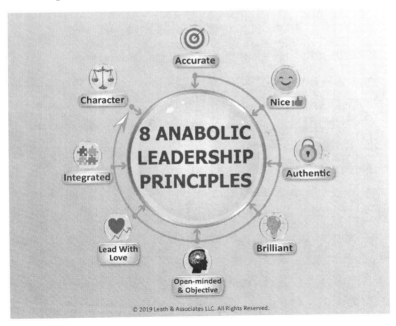

© 2019 Leath & Associates LLC. All Rights Reserved.

"Be yourself, everyone else is taken."
- Oscar Wilde

CHAPTER 9

ANABOLIC PRINCIPLES

Anabolic leaders are... AUTHENTIC

Typically when we think of authenticity, we think of a person keeping it real or keeping it one-hundred percent. But doing so in *all* situations could be detrimental. A YOLO leader has to use prudence in sharing information and consider how it will affect the person who's receiving the information. Equally important is understanding when it's safe to withhold information. There were several times when I chose to be authentic, and people were not ready to receive my input. Authenticity does not always mean that you share everything that comes to your mind about a situation. Still, authenticity evolves when you have proven that the relationship is strong enough for you to share openly and honestly with the person receiving the feedback.

The person receiving the feedback must be comfortable enough to not only accept it, while the person dishing it out must be comfortable saying it. Anabolic leaders give and receive feedback to help others grow. Jack Welch, the former General Electric CEO, is quite arguably one of the best managers in the world because he understood the benefit of giving honest feedback, but also he utilized an open management style that was profound at the time. Jack knew how to connect with people and get them to operate at high levels. I wish I'd learned more about dealing with people early on in my career, and studied Jack's playbook.

Years ago, I was in on a praise and worship meeting of the church I pastored. I felt the meeting went well, and there were good vibes all around. As the meeting was nearing a close, I took the opportunity to critique one of the singer's pitches and style of singing. I spoke out during a time when I thought that I had established a relationship with this person to the point that I could make this statement, we address it and move on. However, the problem was that I used my positional authority as a pastor, but I had not developed the relational authority with this person, so my comment was taken with offense. Then the worship leader shared a few things in an authentic manner that increased the tension in an already awkward situation, and the meeting went downhill fast. Afterward, I realized that I should not have offered my comment to the singer publicly. Instead, I should have provided it in private, and it may have been better received. My disconnect was that I had not established emotional credibility with the person.

Your Truth

There are always buzzwords and catchphrases that a celebrity or someone powerful says that become "golden" in society. Millennials are running with the term "I'm speaking my truth!" I'm still not sure what this means. Yes, Oprah said it a few times, but the saying that there are three sides to a story remains true: i) your version; ii) the other person's version, and iii) the truth. Your truth about yourself or a situation can be completely different from actuality. Have you taken an honest self-evaluation? Did you receive feedback from others?

Often, I don't think most people believe their truth, and they like to use the phrase because it sounds convincing. Living your truth means that you are living your life authentically. If you are a person of integrity, you don't have to advertise or preface everything you say by stating it upfront. Your actions will demonstrate your integrity, not your words. I also believe that using this catchphrase gives people a license to placate or overlook a fault that they are not willing to deal with it. More than likely, it's due to flawed character traits like impatience, immaturity, or selfishness.

We all have blind spots that we should be actively working on to develop and grow. You have to develop both emotional and cultural intelligence to know what to say and when to say it. How can we develop authenticity in our young people? We can encourage and steer them to areas that interest and excite them. In this way, they are being groomed to become anabolic leaders to enter into career fields that align with their values and not just for the money.

Standing Ovation

Leaders who lead themselves from the inside out are living an authentic life. They embody all of the eight anabolic principles of a YOLO leader. One of the first people that come to mind is Tony Dungy. The characteristics that stand out to me about Dungy are humility, authenticity, and realness. He was a former American football player and coach for the National Football League. He was the head coach of the Tampa Bay Buccaneers from 1996 to 2001, and then he became the head coach of the Indianapolis Colts from 2002 to 2008. Dungy's claim to fame was that he was the first black head coach to win the Super Bowl when the Colts defeated the Chicago Bears in Super Bowl XL.

The next person who comes to mind as a YOLO leader is Princess Diana. She was the epitome of class, grace, and elegance, and she lived her life on her own terms. As a member of the British Royal Family, she was the first wife of Charles Prince of Wales and the mother of Prince William and Prince Harry. Diana was a commoner, and although she became a princess, she never lost her connection with the people. That's what made her so alive. The world grieved when she died tragically in a car accident, but her life and memories will remain with us forever.

Without a doubt, I think Michelle Obama is a YOLO leader. As the former FLOTUS and wife to the first African

American President of the United States, Barack Obama, Michelle's grace, strength, and character is one to be admired. Her book *Becoming* became a bestseller in the United States in just two weeks and sold 10 million copies worldwide in less than a year.[32] People of all ages, backgrounds, and ethnicities connected with Michelle's personal story of growing up poor in the inner city of Chicago with hard-working parents. She and her brother studied hard, and both graduated from Princeton University. Michelle went on to become a corporate lawyer, married and started a family, and years later became First Lady of the United States.

Another great leader to point out as the absolute YOLO leader of all time is Muhammad Ali. No one transcends the idea of leading yourself from the inside out than Ali. From the moment in 1966, when he chose not to fight in Vietnam and was kicked out of the boxing league because of his stance, Ali stood tall and firm. He lived his life on his own terms, not just because he wanted to prove a point. He tried to raise dignity for all people but especially people of color. Muhammad Ali was a world champion in and out of the boxing ring and the epitome of a YOLO leader.

Finally, there's Warren Buffett, who quite arguably is one of the most brilliant financial minds of our time. Buffett is a man of humility. He still eats the same breakfast at McDonald's, lives in the same house he purchased years ago, and drives the same car also purchased years ago. Warren Buffett is always on the Forbes list of the top wealthiest Americans and has been for the last decade. Business owners pay top dollar to have lunch with him and pick his brain for advice. All of these individuals are in my mind are YOLO Leaders in every shape, form, and fashion.

For the W...

Sometimes winning or being successful can take the pressure off our real issues. For those of you struggling with identity or competency concerns, winning is like anesthesia—it dulls the pain you're going through. We feel good during the highs, and when the lows hit, they remind you of your situation. The best thing that you can do is get caught right in the middle of it. Go through cycles and learn from them. When the children of Israel were in bondage, God delivered them in cycles of deliverance and sin. We want to live in constant truth that is really our authentic self.

In society, winning is the ultimate end. Victory does not make things right. We measure success by winning and losing. Challenge the fact that winning is the ultimate measure of success. Winning in private yields honor and integrity. Granted, you win the Masters or a sports championship, but you can win with your children, families, and in your job. Be authentic and make success scalable wherever you are, as part of embracing your limits.

YOLO Leader Tips for Authenticity

*Speak up

* Don't be manipulative

*Be open and honest with others

*"Train people well enough
so they can leave, treat them
well, so they don't want to."*
-Richard Branson

CHAPTER 10

ANABOLIC LEADERS ARE... NICE

Nice guys get a bad wrap. Nice women get a bad wrap. We always think that to get ahead, you can't be nice. Niceness is more than being a good person; it is treating others better than yourself. There are over 56 verses in the Bible on doing good to one another, don't slander one another, bear another's burdens, and more. If we apply this mindset into our corporate life, we will see how niceness can be one of our success tools. My wife was thinking about changing careers, and she reached out to people that she knew in the industry, and one of her friends said, "Oh, you're probably not a good fit for this business because it's cutthroat and you're just too nice!" My wife is not a pushover. There is a big difference between being nice and being naive. In other words, "nice" does not mean being a doormat, or Hefty where people can dump out their trash on you.

Being nice means that you see the end goal of your long-term plans and envision where you want to be concerning your current situation. Your focus is on connecting with other people to align in your corner to help you reach your destination. Nice people are well aware that success happens at the speed of relationships, and people who are nice, know how to navigate relationships. After all, the higher up you go, the more it's about liking people and less about abilities and dealing with issues. Instead, you're dealing with people and how they are different in their attitudes and actions, and what you can do to get them on board with your vision.

In a study of cultural competence, findings demonstrated that your IQ is what got you the job, but then your emotional intelligence (EQ) is what will keep you there and why the team will rally behind you. A person with a high EQ thinks about others' feelings, is authentic, controls their emotions and thoughts, shows empathy, and offers encouraging feedback that employees. Not only do you have to have a keen awareness of your feelings and that of others, but you also have to be aware of what's going on in the world from a cultural standpoint to help you find solutions to supporting a diverse team be more productive.

I was conducting an educator training in Livingston, New Jersey and I was getting push back from some of the teachers and a few voiced to me, "We don't care what the person goes through at home, we just want to see how they are in the office, because they have to be productive." I believe most of them missed the critical point of building relationships, which leads to employee productivity and overall job satisfaction. As a leader, you need to know a little bit about a person's home life and responsibilities sitting in a desk near you. I'm not saying get all in their business, but having a general knowledge of what goes on outside of work will help positively build the relationship. Sometimes, it's just nice to be nice.

For example, if a person was generally a good, reliable worker and all of a sudden their work slacked off, they make excuses or started coming in late, you realize there is a problem. Your EQ should tell you that there's something going on here, so let me ask about it in a casual conversation. Chances are, you will find out the reason for the changed behavior, and it's up to you to offer to help so they can get back on track. Being distracted or disconnected from work due to personal challenges happens to all of us. The key is not to get stuck and stay disconnected. Nice people are concerned and empathetic towards others.

After preaching a sermon one Sunday, a member came up to me and said, "Hey, are you OK? You don't seem like yourself." The fact of the matter is that this person was right. I was dealing with several business and family issues, and on that day, my delivery was off, and I kept losing my train of thought. So I was grateful that this person noticed. He took time out to approach me and ask how I was doing. As church leaders, we need to develop an EQ as it relates to our members, but we still need to be intimately involved as well. The old adage is true; *people don't care how much you know until they know how much you care.* So you have to practice care and concern in your interactions with others.

When I used to go back home to North Carolina, I attended Pastor Otis Lockett, Sr.'s church. One time I asked him what is the one thing you wish you could do differently? He said, "You know, I wish I could encourage you and others to spend time with the people. Get to know people. You do all these great things in ministry, and the one thing I regret is that I didn't spend time with the people." That was helpful to me, and I realized that I needed to do a better job in that area. As an anabolic leader, you have to prioritize people and not just projects or deliverables because investment in people produces greater long-term success.

Your EQ allows you to connect and relate to people from multiple backgrounds and cultures. You must be able to adjust and flow on various levels. There's a lot of research done on people with different religious expressions with different traditions, morals, and values. Not only that, we are dealing in multi-generational settings, so as leaders, you have to figure out what is important to the Baby Boomers, Gen X, and Millennials. Baby Boomers are loyal to institutions, and institutionalism was their thing. That's why fighting for country and honor or dignity is a noble thing. Millennials, by contrast, are anti-institutional. They are concerned with the 1% controlling the 99% and are protesting in major cities to fight for what they believe is morally right. You must develop your cultural quotient and emotional quotient as a leader.

Your EQ will go a long way to build stronger relationships. People will trust you and be more open to work or do business with you. Greet people often with kind words. Take time out to get to know those around you. Share knowledge. Thank people. You will soon realize that nice people actually finish first!

*"The devil is in the details,
so pay close attention to them."*

CHAPTER 11

ANABOLIC LEADERS ARE... ACCURATE

Merriam-Webster's Dictionary defines "accurate" as "free from error, especially as a result of care. Exact, conforming to a truth or standard." I guess you're thinking; I'm human, how can I be error-free? You're right. An anabolic leader who is accurate speaks not to perfection, but one who has valid and truthful information at his disposal. Leadership is about trust, and an anabolic leader who can develop, maintain, or sustain trust will be the leader that can gain followers. So how does the YOLO leader who is anabolic maintain accuracy?

An accurate leader must be aware of and not make generalities about events. The more specific you are, the more credible you become. This can be played out in your own life as there are things that you may be aware of and are conscientious to research and study. There is too much at stake, so you don't have the luxury of not being aware or not having the correct information when you are dealing with people. I've found that one thing which can derail your team or cause mistrust in your organization is to have inaccurate information. So the YOLO leader works on being accurate in his personal and professional life.

Accuracy includes truthfulness. YOLO leaders are truthful to themselves and know the areas that they struggle with and need to work on. If you are not accurate and truthful, people will fact-check you and go back to look at records to see if what you're saying is true or false. You want to avoid inaccuracies. As a pastor, I have to be careful not to be inaccurate. If I'm talking with the loved one and there's been a death in their family, if I don't remember or haven't received all of the information when I'm addressing one of our members, I may say something that could be harmless but hurt that person's feelings. I know first-hand that funerals are not the place to demonstrate inaccuracies about the deceased.

I was asked by a friend to officiate a funeral service for the relative of a member of his church. I did not know any of the family. I am always nervous when I read names in public, and I'll write down as much information as I can to make names or places very obvious, so when I'm reading, I'm less likely to mess the name up. Well, not on this occasion. I thanked everyone for joining us to celebrate the life and legacy of Ms.

Halston. The only problem was that the woman's last name was Alston. The family allowed me to get away with calling their loved one Halston three more times, and then someone on the front row gave me the evil eye and blurted out, "It's Alston. Her name is Alston." I was thoroughly embarrassed and apologized. The name was written out; clearly, I just continued to read it wrong. Now, when I perform weddings and funerals, I make sure I get the names correct as people are not forgiving. Yet I need to get it right the first time because it shows that I care about the family and that I am not just the hired help.

Accurate synonyms: *precise, careful, correct, definite, detailed, factual, meticulous, proper, rigorous, scientific, skillful, solid, specific, and systemic.*

Inaccuracy will always devalue your credibility no matter who you are or what you have accomplished in the past. I recall an interview with Anderson Cooper of CNN with U.S. Representative of New York, Alexandria Ocasio-Cortez (AOC). During the interview, Cooper asked her to respond to the criticism that she used fuzzy math and was dishonest in her proposals regarding the tax burden on the middle class of the administration's current plans versus her initiatives. Before this interaction, AOC has been criticized for making factual mistakes or inaccuracies. Cooper went on to cite an article by *The Washington Post* over her fuzzy math of Pentagon spending. AOC said, "Oh my goodness. That is incredulous. It could be one word here or there, but I would argue that they are missing the forest for the trees. I think that there's a lot of people that are more concerned about being precisely factually and semantically correct, than about being morally right!"[33] Therefore, what AOC is saying is that facts, precision, and semantics take a back seat to moral credibility.

YOLO leaders cannot be careless with facts, point-blank. The court of public opinion will not let you get away with misrepresentation. If AOC continues to state mistruths, then she will lose the trust of her constituency. YOLO goes to the heart of who you are. You must care about what you say and do at all times. Too many of us think, "what's the big deal about fudging a number here or there?" Lies and mistruths will add up, and you will not be able to regain that trust again. Accuracy and consistency matter and can cost you more than money in the long run.

Failure to Launch

Back in 1999, NASA lost its $125 million Mars Climate Orbiter probe because of a simple math error. Spacecraft engineers at Jet Propulsion Laboratory failed to convert Lockheed Martin's English system of inches, feet, and pounds to metric measurements when exchanging vital data before the craft launched. Lockheed Martin Astronautics in Denver, designed and built the spacecraft, and provided crucial acceleration data. Still, despite quality control and other systems to ensure accuracy, the elementary error slipped through the cracks.

While we all know the Hubble Space Telescope's capacity to capture beautiful space images is considered a great success, initially, it got off to a rough start.

Not long after the launch in 1990, operators noticed a flaw in the observatory's primary mirror that affected the clarity of the telescope's first images. After NASA investigated the issue, they found that there was miscalibrated equipment during the manufacturing of the mirror. The flaw was one-50th the thickness of human hair, but that minor flaw caused major distortion of images. NASA built a replacement mirror and had it installed a few years later.

Granted, we are not NASA engineers, but the minor inconsistencies resulted in a significant organizational derailment. Billions of dollars, equipment, and time were forever lost. Accuracy is essential, and the old adage says, you've got to measure twice and cut once. Since we are talking about YOLO leaders, it's important to note that success or failure to lead yourself resides within you. NASA placed the blame for the Mars Orbiter loss on a third party. The Hubble Telescope defect was blamed on the mirror manufacturer. However, any failure regarding attention to detail is solely on you—check and double-check yourself.

Preparation "A"

"By failing to prepare, you are preparing to fail."
Not only are accuracy and truthfulness key attributes for the YOLO leader, but preparation is also critical. YOLO leaders should never have a "wing it" attitude. The more you prepare,

the more organized and disciplined you become in other areas. Whenever I give a presentation, I practice several times and go through scenarios to see what will work with a particular audience. I have an internal dialogue where I am not only thinking about my presentation, but I am also doing my best to anticipate unexpected hiccups like technology failures or facility problems. Before I arrive, I have already worked out a few scenarios to buffer the stress of unforeseen issues, and I remain flexible so that I can deal with them. I often speak, so accuracy and preparation are keys to my success. Once I review something seven times, it becomes part of me, and I don't have to refer to my notes. Being prepared keeps you alert and on your toes. You are in the zone and now free to move around the room with confidence.

Another tactic to aid in accuracy and preparation is researching the people you are meeting with beforehand. Connecting with decision-makers is something that the iconic CEO, Jack Welch practices, and it can be a game-changer. Knowing about a person's hobbies, taste in music, the arts, or even a family challenge goes a long way in relationship building. Saying things like, "I heard you have a ten handicap in your game. That's great. I'm still trying to get that good." Adding personal touches like, "I hope your mom is feeling better. I heard she wasn't doing well." Again, knowing about the people you are engaging with endears them to you, and your knowledge beyond the business at hand shows that you care about them, and not just landing the deal.

YOLO Tips

Consider trying out these tips to maintain accuracy:

- Set your alarm clock one hour early if you have a meeting to attend. This will provide additional time to prepare and visualize the outcome you desire. It also can be a great time to meditate and relax with deep breathing exercises for five minutes.

- Get the proper rest the night before and eat a balanced breakfast.

- A study by Best Mattress Brand found that, on average, introverts are less likely to experience quality sleep than extroverts.[34] Which one are you? Sleep is critical to accuracy and alertness, so research ways to help you get a good night's sleep.

- If you are speaking at an off-site venue, arrive early (maybe even the night before) to walk through the facility and your meeting space. Walk the room and go through your presentation to help you navigate the room before going live.

- Make sure your information is correct. Fact check and double fact check if you are presenting statistics, complex information, or sensitive information.

- Keep a notepad or take notes on your phone or electronic device to help you remember names and relevant facts.

- Practice and take breaks in between your times of practice. Have discussions with friends and play tricks to help you remember facts. Work on puzzles, play chess, and other mind-boggling games and activities to trigger memory and accuracy. [35]

*"Your talent is God's gift to you.
What you do with it is your
gift back to God."*
- **Leo Buscaglia**

CHAPTER 12

ANABOLIC LEADERS ARE... BRILLIANT

Today, brilliant seems like a concept that's far-reaching, lofty, or beyond our grasp. We don't use it in modern vernacular as much unless we are speaking of scientific or technological achievements. However, I believe that we *all* can be brilliant. There are times when we shine, and our brilliance shines forth for others to see. Brilliant has to do with light and means very bright, radiant, exceptionally clever or talented. When you think of the word brilliant, these other words should come to mind: accomplished, cerebral, creative, elite, genius, gifted, ingenious, intelligent, inventive, learned, masterly, precocious, scholarly, smart, and virtuoso. All of these words indicate that you have a gift, and you stand out when you operate in that gift.

We are made in the likeness and image of God and come from a unique cut like a brilliant diamond. To be brilliant means to shine and to be all that you were created to be, which is fearfully and wonderfully made.[36] You and I were made to shine. YOLO Leaders lead themselves because they want to shine first and attract people to their light. Some people have "it," and others don't. What is the "it" factor? Craig Groeschel, Founder, and Leader of Life. Church in Oklahoma, wrote a book called, *It* in which the premise is about how we refer to people as either having "it," "not having it," or "losing it." Of course, the "it" factor is difficult to describe, but it's one of those things that you know when you see "it."

The same way you can work on acquiring that "it" factor is the same way you can work on being brilliant. Being brilliant means that you've gotten to the point in your life where you have acquired a great deal of knowledge, and you are continually working on mastering those subjects that are meaningful to you, but you have not fully grasped. Marcus Buckingham and Donald Clifton's *StrengthsFinder*, zeroes in on your *strong* points as a result of completing their personal development assessment tool. Clifton's Strengths Finder Tool uses 34 different strength themes and four domains: Strategic Thinking, Relationship Building, Influencing, and Executing. This exercise is designed to help you identify your "talent themes," which ultimately are your strengths. I call this "Living in the

Zone," where you're just flowing in your gift. Maybe you are a singer, musician, writer, administrator, or educator; no one can compete with you when you are in your zone.

I want to emphasize the point that whatever you do well is the activity that allows your brilliance to shine. There is a lady in my town who is a runner. She is a retired tennis instructor, and I've seen her running around town consistently for years. One day I approached her in the post office and said, "I see you running all the time. Do you run professionally?" She replied, "I used to run with people my age, but they are all out of shape or dead. Now I don't have anyone to run with. Sometimes I run with younger people." I thought, wow, that's interesting! She's brilliant and in her zone when she's running. It immediately brought to mind a scene from the movie *Chariots of Fire*, when Ben Cross, the actor who portrayed runner Eric Liddell, said, "God made me fast. And when I run, I feel His pleasure." Liddell is also quoted saying, "In the dust of defeat as well as the laurels of victory, there is a glory to be found if one has done his best."

You can be in pursuit of brilliance. The more you work towards mastering your gift and paying the price to give it your all, you will see how God flows through you. What flows out becomes the essence of who you are. This is the core of what breakthrough coach, Simon T. Bailey discusses in *Releasing Your Brilliance*. Bailey has decades of experience and branded himself as a "brilliance expert" and even coined the term "brillionaire." He teaches people to rediscover their buried talents to shine.

You don't fall into brilliance. You must practice and embrace your *strong* areas and build upon them. Being brilliant is really about taking what's inside of you, and not viewing it negatively as I'm different, but accepting it as a positive for your brilliance to shine. My good friend, Delano Johnson, author of *Refuse to Live Talented and Broke*, talks about the fact that he was a talented youth growing up in the Bahamas under the leadership of the late Dr. Myles Munroe. Delano was part of a Christian rap group, System 3. He came to the U.S. to be famous and received a Grammy nomination. His dream was to be like Walt Disney. So he immersed himself into graphic arts and became a successful graphics artist around the country. He was extremely talented, but he did not have the resources to thrive. His brilliance was on display due to his talent, and it opened doors to his career. Now, he travels around the globe, promoting his book because he learned to embrace his brilliance.

LOL

"Even the gods love jokes."
- *Plato*

One of the things I learned early on was that I have a sense of humor. Not only do I love a great joke, but I can make people laugh without really trying—it's my superpower. Several years ago, I joined Toastmasters to sharpen my public speaking skills. It was an eye-opening experience, and it helped me to put speeches together, speak clearly, and effectively—say what I mean and mean what I say. It's all about how to engage with people.

At Toastmasters, you are required to give ten speeches, and each speech covers a specific topic and length. I recall doing a speech where I had to convey information. I had to present data on negative information, which was no fun at all. When it was my turn, I greeted the timer, the grammarian, and the audience. I got off to a good start, and I continued to convey in-depth information with negative statistics. Yet the more I spoke, the more the audience laughed. I'm thinking, *OK, I'm really not trying to be funny here people.* I finished my speech and went to my seat, waiting for my critique. Over-all, I received good ratings for grammar, timing, and I kept the audience's attention. However, the critic added, "I've got one critique of your speech. You need to learn not to use humor in this particular type of speech. It just didn't fit right, and if you're giving a serious speech, it is important for you to be serious."

I thought, *OK, I can take my lumps and I'll try to do better next time.* As the meeting progressed, a lady came up from the back of the room and introduced herself as a District Repre-sentative for Toastmasters. She decided to sit in on our meet-ing to hear some of the speeches. She offered comments to the speakers before me, and then when she got to me, she said, "Young man, I want to tell you don't ever lose your humor. Use it because it is something that you have, and you should embrace it." When she said that to me, everything the evalua-tors said to me was a distant memory, and I didn't take any of their critiques to heart. I had a district authority from the organization, encouraging me to use my humor. In other words, embrace my brilliance, that thing that makes me unique.

Anabolic leaders spend time cultivating their brilliance. Ever since that encounter, I work on developing my humor and even watch comedians and comedy shows often. Two comedians who use humor the best are Dave Chappelle and Brian Regan— two different styles of funny men, but they have learned to embrace their brilliance. I now use my humor to communicate with my audience regardless of the size or the information I'm sharing. Humor is like cherry flavored medicine; it's sweet to the taste but effective enough to heal you. Joel Osteen uses humor before he preaches a sermon. It helps him connect with people and break the ice. As an anabolic leader, you will be comfortable and confident in who you are and not afraid to let your brilliance shine through. What's holding you back from shining? You are the light that darkness needs right now.

YOLO Tips

- Take a 30-day social media sabbatical. During your break, take a personal inventory of yourself to discover your brilliance. Consider taking this sabbatical at least three times a year: January, May, and August. By

doing so, you eliminate the risk of your brilliance being dull or tarnished.

- Hire a life coach or connect with an accountability
partner to keep you on track in your pursuit of brilliance.

Diamond in the Rough

A brilliant-cut diamond is one that has several facets so that
its brilliance can shine on every angle wherever the light hits
it. We are all like a brilliant diamond being exposed to several experiences each day. Some experiences lead to growth
while others attempt to hold us back. We have to rid ourselves
of negativity and excess baggage to allow the brilliant light
to outshine our flaws, which may make us feel insecure. Yet
once we are exposed to the endless possibilities of our brilliance and cut off the rough edges of fear, low self-esteem, and
waiting for the perfect time, we can move forward in a natural,
positive flow. Jewelers know that a brilliant cut is designed to
reflect light. The more cuts in the diamond, the more light it
reflects.

It is the glory of God to conceal a matter;
to search out a matter is the glory of kings.
- Proverbs 25:2

This Scripture tells us that God is omniscient—all-know-
ing, omnipotent—all-powerful, omnipresent—everywhere
all the time, mysterious and self-sufficient—does not need

anyone or anything. Yet when a king searches out a matter, he has to resort to his judgment, research, and counsel, but God guides his decisions; therefore, the king is releasing his brilliance. God has permitted you to be brilliant because the world needs more brilliant leaders. Not ones who are arrogant but confident in their decision-making and who they are.

Female Brilliance

The findings of a New York University study on the stereotypes of brilliance as it relates to young girls as early as age six were surprising. Girls become less likely than boys to associate brilliance with their gender and are more likely to avoid activities that require brilliance related to science and math. As parents, educators, and influencers of young people, we need to work to diminish the stereotypes that exist when it comes to intelligence.

Additional research by a doctoral student at the University of Illinois and a professor at New York University demonstrated how early gender stereotypes take hold and point to the potential of the lifelong impact on girls.[37] Also, Sarah Jane Leslie, Professor of Psychology at Princeton University, contributed to this research and stated, "We found that adult women were less likely to receive advanced degrees in fields thought to require 'brilliance.' These new findings show that these stereotypes begin to impact girls' choices at a heartbreakingly young age." More critical, Andrei Cimpian, Professor of Philosophy at Princeton University, added, "Even though the stereotype equating brilliance with men doesn't match reality, it might nonetheless take a toll on girls' aspirations and their eventual careers."[38] What are you doing to encourage your daughters and granddaughters to be brilliant?

I think a big shift that we can do as parents is to teach our young people that brilliance is for everyone, and is not gender-specific. When I think of brilliant women, I think of Mother Teresa, who devoted her life to helping the poor. Then I think of my mother, who was brilliant as it related to her family and household responsibilities. My wife Kamili is brilliant, and of course, the list is extensive. Brilliance and problem-solving skills are needed in every career field. As a YOLO Leader, look for ways to shine your light for the world to see.

- What ideas or thoughts consume your day?

- Where is your passion? What brings you joy?

- What is holding you back from unlocking your brilliance (fear, doubt, loss of control)?

- What three things are you willing to stop doing or change to pursue your brilliance (people, places, or things)?

"Those who cannot change their minds
cannot change anything."
- George Bernard Shaw

CHAPTER 13

ANABOLIC LEADERS ARE... OPEN-MINDED AND OBJECTIVE

For anabolic leaders to be open-minded and objective, they must have a high emotional intelligence quotient to flow as a YOLO Leader. Being open-minded means that you welcome feedback and honest dialogue to create win-win solutions. It doesn't mean that you are a pushover, without values, or operate with guiding principles, but it does mean that you are willing to explore areas that are unfamiliar to you. You should be working with a posture of an open hand as opposed to a closed fist.

Leaders with closed-fists are leaders with closed minds. It demonstrates that you are stuck on one particular belief, and when you have new information, you cannot or refuse to receive it. In fact, you vehemently discount it as false because it does not register in your central way of being.

In John Chapter 3, we come upon a late-night conversation between Nicodemus, a ruler of the Pharisees, and Jesus. Having witnessed Jesus's miracles, Nicodemus still could not understand how a person could be saved and born again.

Jesus said, "You're absolutely right. Take it from me: Unless a person is born from above, it's not possible to see what I'm pointing to—to God's kingdom."

"How can anyone," said Nicodemus, "be born who has already been born and grown-up? You can't re-enter your mother's womb and be born again. What are you saying with this 'born-from-above' talk?"

Jesus said, "You're not listening. Let me say it again. Unless a person submits to this original creation—the 'wind-hovering-over-the-water' creation, the invisible moving the visible, a baptism into a new life—it's not possible to enter God's kingdom. When you look at a baby, it's just that: a body you can look at and touch. But the person who takes shape within is formed by something you can't see and touch—the Spirit—and becomes a living spirit.

"So don't be so surprised when I tell you that you have to be 'born from above'—out of this world, so to speak. You know well enough how the wind blows this way and that. You hear it rustling through the trees, but you have no idea where it comes from or where it's headed next. That's the way it is with everyone 'born from above' by the wind of God, the Spirit of God."

Nicodemus asked, "What do you mean by this? How does this happen?"

Jesus said, "You're a respected teacher of Israel and you don't know these basics? Listen carefully. I'm speaking sober truth to you. I speak only of what I know by experience; I give witness only to what I have seen with my own eyes. There is nothing secondhand here, no hearsay. Yet instead of facing the evidence and accepting it, you procrastinate with questions. If I tell you things that are plain as the hand before your face and you don't believe me, what use is there in telling you of things you can't see, the things of God?

"No one has ever gone up into the presence of God except the One who came down from that Presence, the Son of Man. In the same way that Moses lifted the serpent in the desert so people could have something to see and then believe, it is necessary for the Son of Man to be lifted up—and everyone who looks up to him, trusting and expectant, will gain a real life, eternal life.

- John 3:3-15 (MSG)

As you can see, it was hard for Nicodemus to wrap his brain around this concept. Jesus spoke of being born again—a new birth that comes from heaven and gives us life with a new purpose. When we are saved, there must be a change in our character. Open-minded people can make a shift and thrive in a new environment.

My True North

"My hope is not built on the presidency. My hope is built on the fact that Jesus Christ is Lord, and he is still on the throne."

Any pastor will tell you that pastoring is one of the toughest jobs on the planet, but welcoming and inviting people to have an intimate relationship with God is worth more than anything life has to offer. During my fifth year in ministry in 2012, I lost 50% of my congregation. The entire praise and worship team walked out. I lost all but two leaders, and I was devastated. It was a dilemma that I did not see coming. Do I continue pastoring? Did I really hear God? My wife and I prayed, and we decided to keep on moving. We were in the rebuilding process, and God sent people. I went through more changes than my congregation because I was leading the change. There were discussions from internal leadership about what we should do because although we were growing, it was not enough to sustain the monthly bills.

One of the things that were always in my heart with our church was that I really believe that God called me to pastor in a multicultural church. As we were rebuilding, I kept reiterating that we are a church for all people, not just Black people. Those remarks led to another exodus. Then I realized what I was up against when Donald Trump became President of the United States. It was astonishing. The division, anger, strife, and fear that the people demonstrated let me know the type of people I was leading. Members saw Trump's election as the end of the world. Of course, I was shocked by the turn of events, but there was nothing I could do to change the election results. I surmised, *OK, there must be a lesson that God wants to teach people.*

Admittedly, I was excited when Barack Obama became the first Black President. Yet some of his policies I did not agree with, and in certain circles, it was almost as if I had to because I'm a Black man. Many people expected you to walk lockstep with everything that Obama espoused, but I didn't believe that. But I want it to be clear that my hope is not built on the presidency. My hope is built on the fact that Jesus Christ is Lord, and He is still on the throne, and that's my mindset, point-blank.

During the rebuilding stage, another idea that I wrestled with was pastoring a church that honored my belief in a biblical interpretation as it relates to leadership. I had several leadership adjustments to make because one of the things that were near and dear to me is that we were in the Black community, and male leadership was low. Most of the movers and shakers in the church were women. I love women, and I love how women have held things down to support and strengthen the church, but without strong black men, we would lose as a generation.

I decided to identify and develop strong male leadership aggressively. Right around the time that I was making this shift, I was being open-minded and seeking God's guidance, but my position was not popular or pragmatic. I truly felt a strong conviction that I wanted to honor God and not demean others and to put our community in a place where we saw positive Black males refute what was being portrayed on TV and in the media. I received a lot of push back, and there was another exodus, but this time, I was at peace. I had found my "True North," my internal compass that kept me on track as a leader with my values and beliefs.

As God's timing is always perfect, another opportunity was presented to merge with a predominantly white church on the other side of town. My discussions with the other church started a year prior, yet God was manifesting what He set in my heart all along—I was to pastor a multicultural church. Initially, I still questioned whether I was open-minded? Was I objective? Was I hearing my people? I had to be careful as a pastor not to lead based on emotion but to lead based on internal conviction, which may not be popular.

Before making the final decision to merge, I was meeting with one of my leaders, and he confided in me that he and his wife had never been out to dinner with a white person. I was flabbergasted. After that conversation, I knew that it was time to shift and lead *all* people who loved Christ. We ended up meeting in April of 2018 and had joint services with

Maranatha Christian Fellowship for several weeks. On September 23, 2018, we had our merger celebration, which combined Destiny Church with Maranatha Christian Fellowship, and we officially became Converge Church. We are a multicultural multi-generational, multi-ethnic church. The process of being multicultural is a work in progress. There is a difference between multicultural and multi-ethnic. Yes, we are multi-ethnic, as we have more than one ethnicity represented, yet being multicultural requires us to conduct services that reflect all of the cultures. Although you may have more than one ethnicity going to your church, if the worship experience of each ethnicity is not embraced, then the church is not multicultural.

Through all of the adjustments, I had to ask myself if I was being open-minded and objective. I believe that I was because I didn't make a decision based on any particular group, nor did I decide to satisfy some specific needs. Instead, I made the ultimate decision to move because I felt that it's what God called me to do. I lead based upon my initial vision. If your team does not embrace the vision, then it will not come to pass.

Your Gifts Will Make Room

There's no doubt that we are all talented with unique abilities. How we choose to display our talents is based on the arena that we are most comfortable and one which could lead to our success or mastery in our skillset. As an avid basketball fan, I am intrigued when a young player comes on the scene, which is a product of a successful former NBA player. These past few years, we have witnessed the incredible talent of Steph Curry of the Golden State Warriors, and Seth Curry of the Portland Trailblazers, sons of the great sharp-shooter Dell Curry. The Curry brothers made NBA history for being the first brothers to play against each other in a championship playoff game. Dell Curry and his wife Sonya have remained supportive of their sons throughout their college and professional careers.

By contrast, Lavar Ball, the boisterous dad of three sons—one is in the NBA, Lonzo Ball, and the other two have played overseas. Yet, Lavar continues to garner the spotlight in the media by stating who his sons are better than, how he could have beaten Michael Jordan and other profound statements with no validity. Lavar Ball is a prime example of a father pushing, if not demanding, his kids be great without allowing their gifts to flow. He has stirred up several controversies with other players, teams, and continues to bully those in the sports decision-making arena to make an offer to his other two sons.

Steph Curry honed his craft and worked on the fundamentals at Davidson College, a small college in North Carolina since the larger Division I schools did not see his potential. Steph's rise in his career was a work in progress. When it's your passion, you have to develop for the public in private. By operating when no one else is watching, Curry took the nation by storm when he scored over 30 points in the NCAA tournament in 2008 to take Davidson College to the Elite Eight. Before that, no one had heard of Davidson. It was the epitome of David versus Goliath. It was classic, and Steph became great as a college sophomore.

Steph's rise from obscurity reminds me of King David. As a boy, David tended sheep for his father, Jesse. The prophet Samuel came to Jesse and told him that Saul would be dethroned, and he was there to anoint one of Jesse's sons as the next king. Jesse brought all of his sons that he thought were worthy of being the next king. Like Samuel, most of us assume that anabolic leaders have a specific physical appearance and stature. Yet for anabolic YOLO Leaders, the inside counts a great deal more than the outside. Great leaders have intrinsic values, not just outward qualities. It's not surprising that many attractive people tend to be the most insecure because they focused so much time and attention on building the outside while neglecting the inside. As the familiar story goes, David was anointed king as a small shepherd boy.

In addition, Lavar Ball's actions leave no room for his son's natural gifts to flow and garner the attention of others. Ball's antics make those in authority look the other way as they do not want to deal with his brazenness. Dell Curry has sat back and watched his son's athletic gifts make room for them. We know that a man's gifts make room for him and bring him before great men.[39] Steph Curry has several projects and opportunities provided to him outside of basketball.

From a scriptural perspective, the principle that your gift is not so much a western worldview but a middle eastern custom where gifts were a way to introduce yourself to other people. When Queen Sheba came to see King Solomon, the Bible said that she sent and brought gifts to him, which opened up other opportunities for her. It was customary to find out what the king wanted, and you were to gift it to him upon him granting you a meeting. The scribe would tell the king who was waiting to meet with him and what gifts they brought, and the king would decide if he wanted to meet that person.

Great leaders know how to pull greatness from others. Inferior leaders push and pull to the brink of exhaustion and never allow the person to shine on their own. David became the greatest King that Israel had ever known. Despite his hiccups and challenges, David was still anointed to be a leader and fulfilled the call on his life. Even though we think we are the captains of our destiny, there is a calling larger than us. Are you fulfilling the call on your life? What steps can you take to bring you closer to that path?

Fact vs. Truth

Since we were on the Earth, gravity is a fact and not a truth. Yet if I landed on the planet Mars I would quickly realize that gravity is a fact because I changed my environment. Along the same line of reasoning, if you are broke but you live in New York City, it is a fact. However, if you earned the same salary in Ghana, West Africa, you would be considered rich. Therefore, being broke is not a fact; it is a truth because you changed your environment. You've got to set yourself up in the right environment where you are not afraid to take risks and do what's necessary to get things done.

Open-mindedness is very individualistic. In a church setting, there is this idea of an individual Jesus; I call him the "iJesus." We live in a generation of therapeutic humanistic deism: i) It must be good if it feels right to me, and ii) It must be right, so I become the baseline, the litmus test of what is good, bad, correct, and wrong. The problem with this mindset is that it only takes into consideration one small viewpoint. Why not step back and take a big-picture view and see what makes a town, community, continent, or the world happy. Remember, God spoke to the church at large. He never spoke to individuals or denominations by name. The global challenge is that everyone is so individualistic that they will never find peace if they are grounded in their idea of how life and religion should be. Of course, there is some commonality, and we shouldn't get so caught up in each other's position.

Open-minded and objective leaders empathize with others and try to find merit in their ideas. It is essential to be open and flowing like a river current as opposed to a pond, which is stagnant. The more open you are as a leader, the greater your ability to embark upon new ideas and new ways of problem-solving, as the old way of thinking will not add value to a changing world.

The Liquid Leader

One aspect of being open-minded and objective as a leader means that you can operate at different stages, like water. Water can take on three properties: liquid, gas, and solid. YOLO Leaders have to perform at various stages, as well. You have to be like gas where you let things float away or fizzle out. You cannot address everything as you may turn the situation into more strife than necessary. I've learned as a leader that when facing problems, sometimes a day of letting a problem simmer before I address it is one of the best things I can do. If someone makes a remark towards you or against you, do you respond immediately, or do you let time pass before you answer?

I remember a person commented about me around the time my church, Destiny Family Worship Center merged with Maranatha Fellowship. Someone posted on Facebook that I was uncaring, unloving, and unkind. This person called me everything except what I really believed was part of my character; kind, compassionate, empathetic, pastor, and leader. I had a choice to respond to the post or let it pass. I chose not to respond. The beautiful thing is that people spoke up for me on Facebook, so I didn't have to say a word. Sometimes in a situation like this or otherwise, you've got to be the gas and just let things float away.

In other circumstances, you have to be liquid. That means you can go with the flow. There may be instances where the objective is to get things done, and the way they get done doesn't matter then go with the flow. I remember working in Chrysler Financial, and when we visited dealerships, we had to adhere to our internal standards of the Chrysler Financial floor plan. Chrysler financed the majority of the cars on the lot of a Chrysler dealership. For every vehicle purchased, some proceeds went to the floor plan or to pay off a portion of the lease, and then the dealership got the keep part of that sale as their profit. This procedure was set in stone. Still, we had some dealers who were in locations close to high-density popular cities and other dealers who were closer to low-density towns, so there were rules that we applied, but we learned to be fluid and work out deals with those managers and dealerships. This experience taught me to be flexible and what I found is that I could get more flies with honey than with vinegar. The YOLO Leader, who is objective and open-minded, is willing to go with the flow in some situations. Often when I think of going with the flow, I am reminded of the story of the advice a married man gave to a newly engaged man: "Son, let me tell you this, when you get married you can be right or you can be married. It's your choice." Some people have to be right, and they won't budge, whether in a personal relationship or business. I admit I have a tough time going with the flow because I like being right, but my wife is teaching me that it's better to be married. Learn to be flexible and stay focused on the prize.

Finally, there are times when leaders must take a firm stance and maintain their position. There will be instances where you can't budge, waiver, or change because it would disrupt who you are to your core. There must be some things in your life that are absolute. I know we live in a society where people say, "everything is everything." Yet some things are just right and absolute. One of those absolutes is gravity. It doesn't matter if you agree or disagree with gravity—it's true.

Similarly, in business and other relationships, there should be non-negotiable. By taking a firm position in certain areas, it creates a sense of comfort and a sense of stability, so others will want to continue the relationship with you. It can become a launching pad to try new ideas because it's moving from a place of security and reliability as you have set a standard of core values that will not be compromised. What are your non-negotiables? What are your principles that no matter what, you will not change? Is it the way that you're going to treat people? YOLO Leaders who operate in this anabolic principle of being solid in their position know the set boundaries, and they don't deviate from those boundaries. Take a moment to start with the point of reference on how you view yourself. Are you a person of value? A person of dignity? A person of honor? A YOLO Leader has to operate in either of the water stages to handle the situation. There is an art to doing this, and with time and practice, you will become better at navigating all three phases. Adaptability is the key to being open-minded and objective, and you will be a more effective YOLO Leader.

YOLO Tips

1) Have a clear set of boundaries about what it is that you will and won't do. What areas can you be flexible?
2) What are some ways you can develop the patience to allow things to float away without responding?
3) Identify and create a list of those areas that you will not address in public. Be specific and make sure your team is aware of them.

> *"What does love look like?*
> *It has the hands to help others…"*
> **- Saint Augustine**

CHAPTER 14

ANABOLIC LEADERS LEAD WITH ... LOVE

Anabolic leaders must lead with love. I know you probably didn't expect to pick up a book on leadership and hear the word love. I think that's the problem—we don't talk about love enough. Most people believe that love is an emotion or a feeling. In actuality, love is an action—a verb. Love is expressed by what it does and what is seen by the receiver. Expressing love is challenging in the English language because our words are so limited. Therefore, we tend to have a lot of words with a double meaning. If I say a person is "cool," then the context is important. It could mean a person is cold and lacking warmth or they are cool in a sense that I really like their vibe.

"Love is the ultimate act of acting."

When we look at the word "love," we have to ensure that we know what we mean. Sometimes overuse of the word love loses its power or purpose because it's what everyone else is saying. For example, we *love* our car; we *love* our house, we *love* our outfit, or we *love* our favorite food. The disconnect occurs when you are communicating one meaning and not aware of the implication that the other person attaches to what you said. People hear things based on where they are, not based on what you said.

Love is Pure

When you love, you do so with humility. You need to get to the point where you see the other person at eye level. Have you noticed that disingenuous people can only be nice for a short time? It's easy to fake it to you make it, but in the long run, if it's not in your DNA, it's going to come out and leave the other person hurt. Love seeks to give at the expense of it.

Fruit of the Spirit: 1 Cor. 13:4-7 - Love is patient, love is kind...

Unlike the American English language, the Greek language has several words to define love. They have "phileo" which is a kindly affection for one another. "Agape," meaning unconditional love. There is also "eros" a more erotic, sexual or sensual love, and "storge," which is a patriotic love of country pride that kind of love. As you can see, love has a lot of different meanings, and if you boiled it all down, leaders need to have love in more of a deep concern for others. A leader who loves engages in activities to promote something good. Such a leader is committed to doing something kind and retaliates that type of kindness beyond mere words.

Anabolic leaders enjoy the fact that they are uniquely positioned to help meet the needs of others, so to love means that you put yourself in the greatest position to act. Love is the ultimate act of acting. "For God so loved the world that he gave his son…"[40]This demonstrates that love is active; love gives. God loves mankind so much that he was willing to be mankind to use love to win over death. Unfortunately, many leaders today lead with negative qualities forcing followers to quit or become disengaged.

"A Gallup poll of more than one million employed U.S. workers concluded that the No. 1 reason people quit their jobs is a bad boss or immediate supervisor. 75% of workers who voluntarily left their jobs did so because of their bosses and not the position itself."[41]

What does it mean to lead with love? Love is more than a feeling. Love is an action that encompasses the whole of who you are. When you lead with love, it means not only will you be looking out for yourself, but you'll be looking out for the betterment of others. Leading with love is taking a holistic approach to your life as you are focused on personal growth but also searching for ways to develop those around you. If your company is leading with love, not only is it developing a great product, but it's also enhancing the lives of others by creating a friendly, safe, productive work environment. One of the most devastating things to an organization is when leaders outgrow those that follow them—the leaders become superstars, and everyone else remains stagnant.

Leading with love says that as a manager if I'm reading a book, I'm going to invite those who lead alongside me to read the same book I'm reading. One of the things I love about Pastor George Bowen is not only is a voracious reader; he passes books and articles on to the other leaders often. Pastor Bowen is leading with love as he wants every person around him to grow, not just himself. What is the motivation for leading with love? Such leaders' personal growth must be superseded by their desire to raise others up below their level. This type of active love example is practically played out in Simon Sinek's *Leaders Eat Last: Why Some Teams Pull Together and Others Don't*. Typically, leaders are treated superior and receive unlimited spoils as a result of their position, but there are challenges with being on top. Specifically, when it comes to threats or danger. The team expects the leader to manage such danger in a way that protects everyone on the team even if it means the leader's safety is in jeopardy.

A prime real-life illustration of a leader "eating" last and putting himself in harm's way can be seen in "Miracle on the Hudson," in 2009. Captain Sullenberger was the pilot of U.S. Airways Flight 549 from LaGuardia Airport in New York, headed to Charlotte, North Carolina. A few minutes into the flight, a flock of birds damaged the engines. Sullenberger (Sulley) and his co-pilot Jeff Skiles decided to land the plane on the Hudson River. After a safe landing, water began to rise, Sulley instructed the stewardesses and co-pilot to get on the wings to be in position when the emergency support personnel arrived with boats to assist the passengers. Sulley stayed on the plane until each person got off safely. He realized that as a leader, he was responsible for everyone under his watch, even if that meant his life was in danger. Captain Sullenberger lead with love and put people first. Sulley's selfless act of love to save lives is a reason to celebrate. So to all of my YOLO leaders, if you're going to lead with love, you've got to realize that leading with love is not just in word, but in deeds. You've got to take a hit or the brunt and be willing to sacrifice for the good of the team—that's what leading with love is all about.

1. Do you share reading material with those who work/serve with you?

2. Recall an example where you placed someone else's needs, wants, or desires above your own. How did that make you feel?

3. Name three people's lives you can positively impact this week. Once selected, call or email them, and perform one simple act of kindness (send a gift, post a video, buy a meal, send a card). The focus is the gift, not the amount.

"Leaders must make an intentional change to integrate every area of their lives by being the same person in public and in private."
- Jonathan M. Leath

CHAPTER 15

ANABOLIC LEADERS ARE ... INTEGRATED

Anabolic leaders are totally integrated. What does it mean to be integrated? One word that is similar to integrated is integrity. Integrity means that you say what you mean and you mean what you say. It is one of those qualities that you have to develop over time. Even if you have an opportunity to take advantage of a situation, if you are a person of integrity, you will forgo that opportunity.

Similarly, if you are a person of your word, you will follow through even to the detriment of your self. Integrity does not mean that you only do things that work out for you. When I think of a person of integrity, I think of someone who decides after receiving information that would alter the outcome, and still does what is right!

A person of integrity is integrated, which means that they are the same wherever they are regardless of the environment. When I was working for Chrysler Financial early in my career, I remember this principle so well. As a Christian, I noticed a couple of times when I was getting into situations where I felt the tendency to shrink back and not really say who I was. It was as if I was becoming a chameleon; I changed my outward demeanor to fit the current environment, so as not to be noticed or to stand out. I know there are a lot of people who are like this, either they are chameleon husbands, chameleon leaders, or even chameleon children, trying to fit into an environment that is uncomfortable to them. If you're going to be YOLO Leader, you have to be willing to stand out from the crowd—be different!

After a while, it dawned on me that I didn't want to be a chameleon—I wanted to be a real leader. So I made this simple, intentional change. I decided to be the same in every situation. I decided to be the same at church that I was at work, at home, or just hanging out with friends. I cracked the code and broke the chameleon facade. I had officially integrated my life so that I didn't have to keep up appearances for certain people. I want to encourage you to be integrated and not be a chameleon leader. Be the leader who walks the talk and talks the walk, whether with friends or behind closed doors. You will save yourself the aggravation and embarrassment of trying to keep up with the lies you told somebody else. When you live like this, people can trust you. They can believe that you have integrity in your life and won't let things rattle or shake you, and they can see that you know how to handle the problem and yourself. It's a game-changer!

Years ago, when I was on staff at church, we hired an outside consultant firm to help us with our strategic planning, and we wanted to come up with marketing material to define our church. We spent the entire day with the CEO of the firm to focus on our purpose and make our message clear. We talked about our history and what was unique about our church. We used words to describe us like: authentic, compassionate, committed, devoted, and that we were a ministry of integrity. The consultant wrote out everything on the whiteboard and said to the group, "I want to challenge you with this one word, "integrity." What makes you a ministry of integrity? Are you upfront, honest, and transparent with people about everything?" A few of us chimed in and replied, "Of course!"

The consultant pressed further, "Do you mean that you are going to share and be an open book to every person who asks?" His question made us think about the words that we used to identify our church. After further discussion, we realized that in the process of leading a large organization, everyone is not ready to receive specific information because they are at different levels. As a leader, I would encourage you to have different levels of leadership. You should have an executive leadership team, then specific leadership teams, and then the masses. This way, the information would be shared with leaders based on their level. Information you share with your executive leadership team, you may not share with your general leadership team, and certainly not the masses. You must recognize that people are at different places, and as a leader who walks with integrity, you've got to know how to read where people are. Some people are just not emotionally ready, or they don't have a vested interest in the organization, so sharing information willy-nilly because you want to be transparent may derail your church or business.

People often ask me, "Do I have to tell my spouse everything?" My response is, "How intimately do you want your marriage to be?" Of course, you must set up some boundaries as to what you will tell your spouse. For example, at the outset, you both have to agree that if you are going to be open and honest about everything, it means that you both have to be mature enough to handle what the other person says and not take offense. You should make a covenant agreement with each other and plan ahead of time how you are going to resolve sensitive issues that come up. Being intimate and mature with these types of marital problems takes time, and you must both be willing to take certain risks. Yet if you are totally integrated with your spouse, you should be able to have a stronger marriage.

An anabolic leader who leads with integrity may face missed opportunities. There are some things because you are a person of integrity that may cause others to overlook you: you won't receive an invite to a meeting, the country club or the house in the Hamptons. However, those losses or slights mean nothing because all you have is your name intact! The Bible teaches us that it's better to have a good name than all the riches in the world.[42]

There will be many times in your journey to become a YOLO Leader when you have to face the decision to be popular or be a person of integrity. Yes, sometimes the two can go hand-in-hand, but most of the time, there will be costs to being a person of integrity. Are you willing to pay the price? Be honest with yourself and ask the following questions:

What do I want in my career?

What do I want in my marriage?

What do I want in life?

What am I willing to sacrifice?

Answering these types of questions will be beneficial because everything that you want in life requires sacrifice. Every YOLO leader must make a sacrifice. This could mean that you die to your plans to grow. For example, if you want to have a marriage full of integrity, then you must die to what you thought marriage was going to be. You have to die to allow new things to grow because with every death; there is a new life.

Finally, how will you know when you are walking in integrity? One way to tell is to ask people you trust for feedback. You've got to be willing to hear from them. When you seek feedback, you are permitting a colleague or friend to speak into your life. Although we all fall short, decide to be a person of integrity in every environment so that you move closer to being a totally integrated YOLO Leader.

"Be the kind of leader that others would follow voluntarily, even if you had no title or position."
- Brian Tracy

CHAPTER 16

ANABOLIC LEADERS POSSESS GOOD... CHARACTER

I can't think of a better ending to these eight steps to being a YOLO Leader than to end with character. A great definition of character is "who you are when nobody's watching." In other words, it's not just your public persona, but you are in private is what really counts. I can remember in college at North Carolina A&T State University thinking about what I was going to do with my life. I wanted to be a businessman. At the time, I was in the marketing department, and I served as the president of the American Marketing Association of our chapter in Greensboro. I was also working in student government, and I was a dorm representative. If that wasn't enough to keep me busy, I was a tenor in the award-winning North Carolina A&T State University Gospel Choir, GC!

By sophomore year I received the Dave Richmond leadership award from INROADS, a national organization created to open pathways to get minority students involved in corporate leadership positions. Dave Richmond was one of the Greensboro Four students who sat at a segregated lunch counter at Woolworth's on February 1, 1960, to protest segregation. I was a part of the Raleigh INROADS chapter, and I won the intern of the year award.

I vividly remember growing up on a farm in Elon, North Carolina, where a typical day for us was priming tobacco or what most people call "pulling" tobacco. My family and I were up around 3:30 AM during harvest season that began at the end of summer until mid-September. By 4:30 AM, we were in the fields priming tobacco.

Early on, I learned about hard work and building character from my dad, Reverend Donald Leath, and my mom, Ruthie Mae Leath. One particular summer, I was sitting in the tractor at around 7 AM. I was bored. There were about eight people in the field. I had one job to pull the tractor up. The steering wheel on the International tractor had a spoke in the middle like the Mercedes Benz. I stared at it for a while, wondering if I could stick my head in it and pull it out. I tried the first time, and even though it was a little tight, I pulled my head out. I tried a second time and went a little farther and pulled my head out. Now I was feeling myself, and I tried it again.

Only this time, I went further and let my head touch the instrument panel. I panicked. My head was stuck. I kept pulling and twisting and could not get my head out of the steering wheel. My ears were in pain, and I felt my head swelling. I was terrified. From a distance, I heard, "Hey, pull the tractor up. Pull the tractor up, Jon!" My first thought was that I could pull it up, but I couldn't see. I didn't answer.

My dad came to where I was and saw me struggling. Instead of him covering me like he should have to save my reputation, he called out to the others, "Hey, look at this boy! He done got his head stuck in the steering wheel!" Everyone rushed over to see and were laughing hysterically. My big ears were part of the problem. I still recall my dad saying, "Alright, boy, relax your head. Just relax your head." I kept saying, "I can't get out, I can't get out. My head is swelling!" I turned off the engine. "OK, Jon, we have to figure out a Plan B." I could hear my two brothers laughing in the background. It's a good thing there were no cell phones back then because my video would have gone viral with thousands of memes. "Jon, relax and pull a little bit harder." He was pushing my head from the side near the instrument panel. I broke free! I can't describe the freedom I felt that morning with my dad helping me get unstuck. Whenever we are together, my dad tells this story and emphasizes how big my ears were. Although it is funny and embarrassing, these stories and the hard work on the tobacco farm helped shape my life and taught me during my adolescent and teenage years, the real meaning of character.

I shared this story because I did not want to sugarcoat my life, but I wanted to demonstrate that I developed character through hard work, and there is no getting around that fact. Many people want to take shortcuts or "beat" the system, but you can't. Character counts when you're filling out your expense report. Character counts when you are on a business trip, and you're in the hotel lounge, and you're getting something to drink, and there's another woman in your view who is not your wife. You think to yourself, *No one knows me here. I have my own room. It's cool; no one will ever find out.* Wrong. Character counts when no one's watching. Character counts when you are taking a test, and the last question stumps you, but you notice out of your peripheral vision that the person sitting next to you has the correct answer to that question. You feel the adrenaline rush because you can see their paper as plain as day, and the teacher is not looking. What would you do?

Character is who you are when you're at home on your computer, and no one else is around. As a follower of Jesus, I believe that God is always watching and sees everything. I know when I did wrong things, I didn't want to get caught, but I had this keen sense that I was always in someone's view, and I know who that someone was. Being a person of good character is not just for you but for your family legacy, your sons, and your daughters. What kind of legacy are you leaving for your grandchildren? Don't let your selfish ambitions tarnish your name for generations.

I made a point to emphasize to my team that they had to provide honest, accurate information on their reports. Not only did I want my team to know I was a person of good character, but I also wanted my superiors to know as well. I was in a meeting with our team leaders, and I approached my direct leader right after the meeting and said, "You know something, Eric, you'll never have to worry about my team and me because I realized that my job is to make you look good. We're not going to fudge the numbers." I tell you, I don't know what he was thinking that day when I spoke to him but the expression on his face I could see that it blew him away. So if you go to your boss tomorrow and you tell him or her, "Listen, my job is to make you look good," that will blow them away. Try it, and I believe you're going to open up so so much for yourself. When you're a person of character, you never lose anything.

This world needs people with real character. I've always wanted to pour into the lives of young people, Gen Z. Since they are our future, we need to help them navigate through life. Looking back at the generations, the Baby Boomers were the ones who were stable. They were the greatest generation, and they gave birth to Gen X, the "all about me" generation. Gen X is the one who rebelled against authority. They had children, and Gen X's children are Millennials, the generation who pushed back against authority. Unlike the Baby Boomers who believed in institutions, Millennials think that institutions are corrupt and believe in individualism and self-expression. How do we make the leap to help Millennials and Gen Z understand what it means to be people of character? I think character is lost, so we need to teach character and operate with this in mind.

Once I graduated from Philadelphia Biblical University, which is now Cairn University, I received a Masters of Science Degree in organizational leadership. My thesis was on mentorship as a leadership development tool, and training was always big to me. Shortly after I graduated, I wanted to start a mentoring program. I used to go to Perkins Restaurant, and the breakfast menu offered the "Tremendous Twelve." Yes, it was a lot of food as you had a total of twelve items on your plate: three eggs, four buttermilk pancakes, choice of hash browns or breakfast potatoes, and choice of four bacon strips or four sausage links. I liked that name, so I thought about developing a mentoring program called "T12," I wanted to train 12 individuals on navigating various aspects of life, including finances, relationship building, and leadership. Although T12 never really got off the ground, in 2010, I developed DiscoverHOPE, a Community Development Corporation. A few years later, in 2013, I launched my first training and mentoring program and called it "Character Camp," where during the summer, I provide young people with the skills and tools to become competent individuals and leaders.

The goal of my Character Camp is to make young people better individuals since they are already leaders; we want to build upon their character. I had eight students the first year, and the attendance has doubled year over year. We teach necessary skills like how to choose the right friends, how to make decisions, how to communicate, how to defuse a situation, how to put others first, the benefits of delayed gratification, and money management. Overall, we also want them to take away the notion that being kind to others is a critical component to building character.

I beamed with joy when I overheard Karen, a grandmother of three kids in my Character Camp, saying that her grandkids look forward to coming to Character Camp. It was their second year attending. All four of my children are involved in the camp: my daughter Jael is Co-Camp Director, my sons Jonathan and Joshua are in charge of logistics and gaming, and my youngest Joel, serves as the camp mascot. Even my wife, Kamili, serves as a volunteer instructor. In 2019 we hired teenagers to run the camp, and now all I do is provide the direction. Serving others is one of the noblest callings that you can have, and if you are a YOLO Leader leading yourself from the inside out, then you will become a person of character because character counts when no one is watching.

Back in 2004, I took a trip to Ghana, West Africa. I was there to teach a local pastor about business ethics. As we were driving to our hotel, we stopped at the money exchange to get local currency. I had $100 that I wanted to exchange. At that time, the exchange rate for a Ghanaian Cedi was 0.91 to one U.S. Dollar. So I gave the lady my $100 bill, and she gave me back a hundred thousand Cedis. I knew I was supposed to get back 91,000 Cedis. I got back in line the long line, and I finally get to her window, and I said, "I think you made a mistake and gave me too much money back." She replied, "Oh no, I didn't."

I repeated to her two more times, then finally I counted it in front of her. By now, her attitude changed, and she said, "Oh no. I have made a grave mistake." She was very appreciative. I did not want her cash drawer to come up short because she would probably have had to pay it back from her pocket. I thought to myself, *Jon, you could have just gotten back on the bus, and no one would have ever known because you're only visiting the country for four days.* Yet I realized that character was who I was when no one was watching. I couldn't keep the money because it wasn't mine. On top of that, I was there to teach other pastors about integrity, so I believe it was a Divine setup, and it was a test, and I passed the test.

After that incident, my resolve grew stronger, and I committed to being a man of strong character. In doing so, I made the decision not to take credit for things I did not do. Nor would I take advantage of any person based on my position of authority. If you're a person of character, people can trust you because the end of the day character boils down to trust. Can you be trusted? People want leaders they can trust. They want leaders who lead with love. Leaders who are noble, nice, authentic, accurate, brilliant, open-minded, and objective and integrated. Do you want to know a secret? Someone is always watching. If you are a parent, you'll see yourself in your kids. If you run an organization, you'll see your personality in that organization. If you manage anything, your character comes out and will be on full display. When you learn to lead yourself from the inside out, you've crossed over into living the YOLO Leader life. No matter what challenges come your way, strive to be a YOLO Leader of good character.

Part III

YOLO Master

7 Types of People You Need in Your Life

CLERGY
Someone who can speak to God for you and remind you to speak to God for yourself.

COACH
Someone who instructs or trains you.

CHAMPION
Someone who will fight for you or argue on your behalf.

COUNSELOR
Someone trained to give you guidance on personal, social and psychological matters.

CONFIDANT
Someone with whom you can share your secrets.

CHALLENGER
Someone who engages in a contest or against you or is your rival.

CRITIC
Someone who judges the merits of your actions or accomplishments with the goal

© 2019 Leath & Associates LLC. All Rights Reserved.

"You need to associate with people that inspire you, people that challenge you to rise higher, people that make you better. Don't waste your valuable time with people that are not adding to your growth. Your destiny is too important."
- Joel Osteen

CHAPTER 17

7 PEOPLE YOU NEED IN YOUR LIFE

When we look at the framework of becoming a YOLO Leader, one aspect that you cannot overlook is having a strong team to support your growth. Everyone needs a support group of people in your life that can see areas that you cannot see. For YOLO Leaders who seek to be game-changers, first, you must be keenly aware of your internal qualities, second, you will need to assemble a team to ensure that you are pursuing your best and highest self. I heard a story of a successful young man who had many friends, and he went to see a wise man to ask him questions about life. The burning question that he had in his heart was, "How many friends do you need in life?" The wise sage said, "Son in life really all you need are seven friends." The young man responded that he had hundreds of friends. The fact of the matter is that the quality of your friends count, not the quantity.

Who are the 7 People You Need in Your Life?

The first person that you need in your life is a coach. A coach instructs you on how to perform better. Tiger Woods was asked by a reporter, "Why do you have a coach?" Tiger replied, "Because I can't see myself swing." Again, everybody needs a coach. Michael Jordan needed a Coach, Steph Curry, one of the greatest shooters of all-time needs a coach; Serena Williams, an elite women's tennis champion, needs a coach.

The second person that everybody needs is a counselor. This is a person who is trained to give guidance on personal, social, and psychological matters. In our world, people are working harder and setting bigger goals. They're achieving more, yet we're seeing people hit a wall. Recently a prominent pastor who had mental illness committed suicide just two hours after performing the funeral of another young lady who committed suicide. With mental illness awareness on the rise, a trained counselor can refer you to a therapist or help you better manage your well-being. My sister-in-law, Dr. Nancia Leath, focuses on the importance of self-care and helps people get into the habit of taking care of their mind as well as their bodies. It seems everyone is juggling so many things and running ourselves too thin. I know many people don't see the need for a counselor, but you need someone to help you stop, slow down, and sharpen your saw.

I believe the next person you need in your life is a **critic**. This is a person who is skilled at pointing out areas in your life where you need to get better. Don't overlook or devalue the voice of your **critic** because, with every piece of criticism, there is some truth in it to help you succeed in life. Your critic will keep you on your toes, which we all need.

Next up is the **challenger**. We all need a **challenger** in our life—that person who we are competing against in our own right. This is someone who has achieved something that you desire to achieve. It's OK to chase after someone as you are trying to achieve greatness. Having an example of a preferred path gives you a mental picture that you can do it too. This person is your rival, and you always have your eye on them. Your goal is to be better than this person, so it means that you are challenging yourself to get better. If anything, this person is the catalyst to launch you into the person you need to be. Everybody needs a **challenger**; the greatest sports team can only be great if they have a great opponent. You cannot do great things unless you're facing an equally great opponent. They make you go to the gym earlier and make you stay up later, sharpening your proposal or your skills. Be prepared; your **challenger** will eat your lunch, so you've got to be on your "A" game. Unless you know your competition, you won't know the skills you need to develop. Your **challenger** wants the same thing you want...to win. Who wants it more? The choice is yours to make.

The next person you need is a **confidant**. Do you have a **confidant**? If not, you need one. We all need a special person in our life to share our secrets, that hidden part of us that we don't want anyone else to know. Your **confidant** is a friend you can trust who will not spill the beans, not ever. Any revelation of your secrets could turn your life upside down. I think the exciting thing about sharing those deep secrets with your **confidant** is that releasing it gives you freedom from whatever those secrets are doing to bind you up or to keep you from moving ahead. So it's good for you to vent to someone and share your frustrations and let your hair down without judgment or other consequences. Most of the time, we have to be "on" and don't get to be ourselves in specific settings, so having a safe space to talk and share will be beneficial to your health and well-being.

Another essential person you need in your life is a **champion**. Everybody needs a **champion**, a person who fights or argues for a cause or they fight or argue on your behalf. You need someone who is listening out for your name, and if words spoken about you are not true, then it's your **champion's** job to call them to the carpet. Realistically, you cannot be everywhere, so having someone you trust in certain circles to speak well of you is vital. The Greek word to speak well of someone or to praise is eulogeó. This is where we get the word "eulogy" from "to speak good words." We usually hear eulogies when someone passes, but your champion speaks them while you're alive! Make sure you have a true **champion** in your inner circle of friends.

Last, but certainly not least, everyone needs a member of the **clergy** in their friendship circle. This is someone trained to speak to God on your behalf, but they also encourage you to do the same. Many people don't think they need a **clergy**, but we need someone to keep us grounded and remind us of our God-ordained purpose. Psalm 139 says that we are fearfully and wonderfully made, which means that all of us have a purpose on this Earth; none of us are accidents. I want to encourage you to find a member of the **clergy** and get connected to a church, small group, or other fellowship connected to God.

To recap, the seven people that you need in your life are **coach, counselor, critic champion, challenger, champion**, and **clergy**. Each one serves a specific purpose to help you grow into an exceptional YOLO leader.

YOLO Tips Exercise

- Write down the name, email, and contact number of the seven people in your life who fill these roles. If you do not have someone in a specific function, you need to find someone soon. If you have more than one person to fill a category, then consider it a blessing. Your assignment is to keep going until you have all of the roles filled and then share your list within that circle.

Note: You do not need to tell anyone your "critic" or "challenger." As long as you know who they are, that's enough.

*"Work on yourself more
than you do on your job."*
- Jim Rohn

CHAPTER 18

MASTERING YOUR
HEALTH & WELLNESS

Now that you've come to the end of this book, look at it as the beginning of a new journey. In 2 Peter 2:19, it says for whatever overcomes a person, to that he is enslaved. Another way to put it is that you are a slave to whatever has mastered you. To master means to have control or authority over, so taking steps to become a YOLO Leader is designed to help you have control or mastery over your life. YOLO Leaders do not leave their life goals, accomplishments, or well-being up to others; they control it themselves.

As a life coach, I encourage people to stop letting life control you, but you control your life. You must control the things that you have control over. A few lines from The Serenity Prayer brings this point home:

> *God grant me the serenity*
> *to accept the things I cannot change;*
> *courage to change the things I cannot accept;*
> *and the wisdom to know the difference.*[43]

YOLO Leaders know the difference between those things that they can change and have the ability to change, and they know the difference between what they have to accept. Just think about it, you've already spied out the land and see the terrain you want to conquer, and now you have to make a decision: Are you going to be mastered by things that happened in your past? Maybe a setback occurred in your life years ago, such as a divorce, loss of employment, overlooked for a promotion, or a severe illness, and it made you feel like a failure. I believe situations come into your life for one reason; to push you to the next level. Most of you wouldn't go unless you had to. When you learn to adapt to change, you are ahead of the game because a key to life is changing before you have to! Chances are, if you have to change, then it may already be too late, but I believe that you can teach an old dog new tricks. Hang in there.

How Much is Enough?

When I think back to my early college years as a business major, I wore business suits and carried a briefcase every day. I thought I had it all figured out; make a lot of money and die with the most toys. I bought into this way of thinking as it made sense, especially for a boy who grew up on a tobacco farm. All of my business major peers were vying to get an interview with a pharmaceutical company. Back then, pharmaceutical sales jobs were paying $50,000 a year plus bonuses *and* a car. I wanted that type of job badly. Many top companies came to our school to set up interviews. I was excited to get an interview with Merck. I had prepared as best I could and tried to remember techniques to connect with the interviewer by having a shared interest outside of the job. I interviewed with a guy who wore a bow tie. I don't wear bow ties, and I could sense in the interview that we didn't have much in common. Merck never panned out. Fortunately, I had an interview with Chrysler Financial. I thought I was big time. Here I was a country boy going on my very first real big-time interview with Chrysler Financial out of town. I went to the initial interview at school, and it went well, so they invited me to the next interview. The letter said I was going to be picked up by Connecticut Limousine. I thought to myself, *man; you have arrived.* I told my brother, "Man, I'm going to interview for this job up in Connecticut, and they're going to pick me up in a limousine!" I bragged to all of my classmates about my interview in Connecticut.

My flight was great. I came down the escalator, and a guy was holding a sign with my name written on a plaque. "Are you Jonathan Leath?" The man asked. "Yes, sir!" I said. He took my bag. I'm thinking, *wow, this is really nice.* We walked out of the airport sliding doors, and he pointed me to his 24-passenger shuttle bus with the name "Connecticut Limousine" written across the doors. I was disappointed. I didn't want a bus. I wanted a limo! I had visions of a black stretch limo with caviar, crackers, and sparkling apple cider waiting for me inside. Instead, all I got was a bottle of water and a bumpy ride to the hotel. Oh well, the hotel was beautiful, and the concierge person asked me what size bed I preferred. "I'll take a king-size bed."

When I walked into my room and saw this huge king-size bed, I was like a kid at Christmas. I unpacked my bag and ordered room service. I put on the plush white robe and laid across the bed and watched T.V. At bedtime, I slept sideways on that bed that night because it was so huge. I was used to sleeping in a twin bed that I shared with my older brother. The interview went great. I was on Cloud 9—you couldn't tell me anything. When I got back to school, I acted like it was no big deal as if I already had the job.

Once I accepted the job offer, I started thinking about how much money I was going to make. I began to measure success by money. I didn't have a good idea or perception of how much was enough. I thought enough was enough to buy what I wanted and send some home to mom. During that time, having enough took on a new meaning. Years later, I learned that real success has little to do with money and more to do with purpose. I listened to a speech that Professor Deepak Malhotra of the Harvard Business School gave to the MBA graduating class of 2002. He talked about how he bought into the myth that pursuing money was the highest goal and that making a million dollars before he turned thirty was his goal. Malhotra focused on making money and went from having $2.26 in his bank account to 2 million dollars in five years. He thought being rich was the key to happiness, yet he realized that chasing money is not what life is all about, nor is it the measurement of success. He realized that he sacrificed a lot to chase money. What are you willing to sacrifice to get money? In investing, there is a term called "opportunity cost" It is the cost you pay in missed opportunities. Opportunity costs could be missed birthday parties, broken relationships, or missing significant life-changing memories. In my line of work, I meet people at all stages of life. To this day, I have never met a person on their deathbed tell me, "I wish I made more money." Instead, they all tell me, "I wish I had more time to spend with my family."

Financial Awareness

It is hard to take financial advice from a CPA who files bankruptcy or trusting a barber who desperately needs a haircut or choosing a mechanic who drives a broken down car. Leaders are required to operate at a higher level—especially if they want to gain the respect of others in their field. For those leaders who have mastered their finances in their personal lives, they tend to treat their organization's resources like they treat their own. The Bible says, "Money answers all things."[44] How well are you administering God's answers to your problems in your personal life?

Before Kamili and I got married, I never bounced a check. I was on top of my finances and knew where every penny went. Once I got married, all that changed. I began to rack up so many bounced check fees that I had to declare a moratorium on spending. Kamili and I had a "come to Jesus meeting." What we failed to do was share our financial goals and desires at the beginning of our marriage. Feeling the consequences of bounced check fees was enough pain for me to realize that we had to get on the same page. Communication is the key to our marriage, and we were able to get our financial house in order, and within a few months, we were on a better financial footing.

What messages are you telling yourself and others about money? Do you see money as a tool or as a commodity—something to be gathered and stored? Is money something that you use to build up the Kingdom of God, or do you use it as a sign of God's abiding presence in your life? YOLO Leaders understand the direct correlation of how to manage money and how to lead themselves. YOLO Leaders have mastered the art of financial stewardship and use the power of leverage and liquidity. They don't live to the hilt. Instead, they live within their means while providing a level of safety and long-term security for the future.

YOLO Tips
1. Get a money plan that works for you and stick to it.

2. Have a regularly scheduled family finance meeting.
3. Practice generosity with your time, talent, and treasure.

Charting Your Course

I recall hearing a story of a cruise ship captain talking to a person who ran a jet ski shop. The owner of the jet ski shop was talking about how agile his jet skis could make quick changes and turns regularly. The cruise ship captain said to him, "I can't make changes that fast. I can't just make a decision and then turn my ship around. I have to plan my moves a few days beforehand." Within earshot of this conversation was the captain of an aircraft carrier whose ship was the length of eight football fields. He said to the cruise ship captain, "Yes, you have to plan your moves days in advance, and when you change your move, you have to notify the crew members in advance." Then he said to the jet ski owner, "You can make changes in your direction instantaneously, but my decisions have to be made at least a month in advance because my vessel is so big."

I make this ship analogy because depending on the position that you have as a business owner, entrepreneur, or even if you haven't started a business yet and are still on your job, you can be agile to make decisions about your future. Most start-up tech companies can make moves fast, but when you are an established business, your steps have to be more calculated. If you have been in management for a while and you want to make a shift to becoming a business owner, do your due diligence first, especially if you have a family. Even if you're the owner of a corporation and you want to change things up, you have to calculate those moves differently. Whatever stage you are at in your life and career, as you're becoming a YOLO master, consider various outcomes before you make a move and speak with your counselor and your coach two of the "7 People You Need in Your Life."

If you are at a place where your family is well taken care of and you have grandchildren and retirement is in front of you, and you're saying to yourself, *What's going to be my final act? What am I going to do now?* Now it's time for you to go back and find other leaders and pour into their lives. At this stage in your life, you've learned how to take breaks and take time to enjoy your successes. By now, you should be connected with a community of people who can help bring out the best in you. One of the best ways to find joy and fulfillment in your life is by pouring into the next generation.

We are facing a leadership crisis. The current Baby Boomers are 60 and above and are retiring, which means that the most substantial economic shift in history is about to occur. I recently read an article that said that Baby Boomers would put nearly 21 million homes on the market and create a tidal wave of homes for sale.[45] Who will buy them? The next generation has to be financially and mentally prepared to step up to the plate. Therefore as YOLO masters, don't just clock out—check back in...this generation still needs you. This is the most productive time in your life to invest in others to pass the mantle. You may also find true fulfillment and finally accomplish those tasks that you've been putting off for the longest.

This is also a time for a spiritual health check. Find out where you are and where you stand in your faith. I'm a person of faith, so I believe that God is my Creator and that God created me for a purpose. Once you have a firm position, you can recalibrate where you are on your YOLO journey. A few things to keep in mind:

i)   Keep yourself in community with people that can spur you on that are pushing you. These are your coaches, champions, counselors, clergy and even your challengers ;

ii) Engage in a wellness community to teach you to meditate, yoga, swim, or if you are distracted, unattached, learn ways to focus on your inner self. Consider the last time you totally shut yourself off from all technology. This can be a time to incorporate a technology fast into your health check. You can abstain from certain online activities. For instance, Monday is your technology fast days, and that's where you decide no Facebook, Instagram, Twitter, or any other social sites for the entire day. Instead, devote that day for quiet time, taking a walk, or watching nature;

iii) Create boundaries and time for people who matter. If you're married, spend time with your spouse, if you have children, spend time with them, if you love nature or pets, enjoy that time. Be intentional with those who matter because your interactions will be beneficial in maintaining your spiritual health, and

iv) Be open and honest with your counselor and confidante about your mental health. Most of us are in high-stress environments, and we need to speak up and ask for professional help when we feel overwhelmed. In the U.S., 40 million adults have some variation of an anxiety disorder, which is the most common mental illness.[46] What most people don't realize is that anxiety disorders are treatable, yet only a small percentage seek treatment. Another point about anxiety disorders is that they develop "from a complex set of risk factors, including genetics, brain chemistry, personality, and life events."[47] Reaching out and seeking help will put you in a better position to achieve your YOLO Master goals.

Final Self-Awareness Check

Early on, I talked about embarking upon a real self-awareness discovery of yourself. To do that, you have a few tools at your disposal. You can start with the DiSC Personality Profile, which measures your behavior in certain situations. You can also use the Johari Window, which allows people to look at you while you, in turn, see yourself from different viewpoints, and finally the 360 Degree Feedback, where you seek honest feedback from your colleagues, subordinates or superiors.

For any actual growth to be effective, YOLO Leaders must take off the mask and be vulnerable and authentic. Since everyone wants to be liked, there is a risk of authenticity. Who knows? Your authenticity may offend someone, or you may be offended by someone else's authenticity. However, a YOLO Leader understands the power and the benefit of being authentic because if you want someone to be truthful with you, then you must be open to receive what they have to say, and allow the true you to show up. If "your representative" shows up, then the chances of seeing results or benefitting from these behavior and personality exercises will not happen.

I want to challenge you as a YOLO leader in the area of personal growth and personal development to be authentic in spite of the risk of being offended. You must choose not to be offended. What would you think if I told you that you don't have to be offended in your life anymore? Wouldn't it be great if you could offense-proof your life? How can you do that? Quite simply, choose *not* to be offended because offense is a choice. When you choose to be offended, you're giving another person power over your attitude and eventually over your life. In essence, you've given them the access to change your mind, change your emotions, and make you feel a certain "less than" kind of way. Don't give away that power. Remain in control of your circumstances. Authentic people avoid those who make them think and feel negatively about themselves.

Remember, you have to choose not to be offended. You have a split second to either receive that offense and make it true or choose not to allow it to take root in your mind. In Dr. Caroline Leaf's book, *Who Switched Off My Brain*, she talks about the science behind how our brain responds when we receive bad news or negative news. Neuroplasticity is the ability of the brain to change continuously throughout a person's life. Based on how the brain works, there is a split-second or short window of time where we can receive that information as true, or we can reject it as false. If we choose to accept it as true, then our brain engages in synaptic pruning, deleting neural connections no longer necessary. These connections form around that negative thought. If we reject it as false, then that particular thought never has an opportunity to take root in our life. So when we are authentic and real, we must not give away our power and be offended. In Psalm 119:165, it says, great peace have those who love thy law, and nothing shall offend you or nothing shall cause you to stumble. Choosing not to be offended, and leading yourself first is one of the greatest gifts you can receive.

As you are becoming a YOLO Leader, always know that there is always room for growth. In actuality, each time you get rid of an old way of thinking, you can stretch your brain to receive new information. Our brain has growth potential and is always growing and expanding. When we get older, our brain slows down, growing at a specific rate, but it still has growth capabilities. As a YOLO Leader, I've learned to reprogram my brain around negative things that happened in my past. You can too! While I can't forget my past, I don't have to continue to give it the power to control my future.

"The secret of change is to focus all of your energy not on fighting the old, but on building the new."
- Socrates

CHAPTER 19

THE LIFELONG JOURNEY BEGINS

So, what's next for you? After reading this book, hopefully, you've been thinking about yourself in a whole new way that you never dreamed was possible. Now, I want to challenge you to lead past your comfort, to lead past the convenience of the everyday mundane, and to embrace the mantle of the YOLO Leader because the world needs more of us.

Leading yourself starts with small gestures that have larger, long-term results. The next time you are sitting in a meeting, and no one speaks up or takes control of a mistake or a problem; you be the one to speak up. The next time you witness the mistreatment of another person, regardless of the situation, you should be the one to speak up. The next time you face an unpopular decision that you know deep down inside is right, you should not waiver on your position. The world is full of "keyboard bandits." These are the people who sit back in the comfort of their own home. They are removed from the shrapnel of everyday living and the complexities of leading any small, medium, or large endeavor and choose to use their avatar to play "Monday Morning Quarterback" to all of the people who are actually out on the field. There is hope for them; however, unless they muster the courage to come out from behind the shadows, they will never reach their fullest potential.

YOLO Leaders don't hide behind excuses. If they try something, and it fails, they take responsibility; they take the heat. What would this world be like if there were more YOLO Leaders? How many marriages would be saved if both spouses decided to die to their own way and begin living to out-serve one another? How many businesses would thrive if employees started to see the company they work for as their own, realizing that their efforts affected the bottom line? How many students would be motivated to excel in school if they realized they would be judged not by their parent's connections or social standings but by their individual efforts? What would happen is everyday people began to see their community as their extended family and decided to put aside their differences and embrace their commonalities? Although it sounds cliché, I think the world would be a much better place.

Next Steps

We need a YOLO Leader Army. Today, I want to invite you on the journey of a lifetime. I want to challenge you to do the following:

1) Reread this book, except this time, read it with the idea that you want to change at least one thing in your life. Maybe you want to work on one of the 8 Principles for anabolic leaders, or perhaps you want to find and develop more substantial relationships with five of the "7 People You Need in Your Life. You could also revisit the "Old Leadership Model" behavior and embrace the "YOLO Leadership Model." Whatever you decide to do, just run with it!

2) Share the YOLO leadership concept with someone you know is ready to become a YOLO Leader.

3) Write your own story—it's already in you. The fact that you are reading this book today is because one day, I decided that it was time for me to become a YOLO Leader.

The late great John F. Kennedy was known as an innovative leader. While he had flaws as all of us do, there was one thing he was able to accomplish. He rallied the country around a single idea –send a man to the moon before the end of the decade. On May 25, 1961, President Kennedy addressed Congress and the world, sharing his dream to land a man on the moon. In his speech, he pointed out two critical facts, 1) we had the resources to do it, and 2) we had the intellect to do it.

It was also President Kennedy who, earlier that year during his inauguration, said something that I will never forget. It's a motto that I live by and an underlying principle of the YOLO Leadership model. He said, *"Ask not what your country can do for you ask what you can do for your county."* The YOLO Leader is not looking for a handout but is willing to lend a hand to help lift others up. Now that you know who you are and you have what it takes, the thing that was stopping you no longer has the power to control you—you now control it. Today is the first day of the best days of your life because you have learned that before you lead others, you know the importance of leading yourself because, in the end, **You Only Lead One.**

#YOLO Leader

AUTHOR BIO

Jonathan **M. Leath,** MSOL, is the co-pastor of Converge Church a thriving, multi-cultural, multiethnic, and multi-generational church in Moorestown, NJ. He is also the founder and CEO of Leath & Associates, LLC and a Life Coach. Jonathan serves as the Executive Director of DiscoverHOPE CDC, a youth leadership and development organization that helps young people develop their character and cultivate integrity. He and his wife, Kamili, have one daughter and three sons. For more information visit www.jonathanleath.com.

RESOURCES LIST

As a YOLO Leader being a continuous learner will help you along the journey. The following books have helped me become better.

1. **The Bible** (New King James Version)
2. **5 Levels of Leadership**, Maxwell, John, C.
3. **Turn the Page**, Parker, Dr. Johnny
4. **7 Habits of Highly Effective People,** Covey, Stephen, R.
5. **The 4 Disciplines of Execution,** McChesney, Chris., Covey, Sean., Huling, Jim.
6. **The Ideal Team Player,** Lencioni, Patrick.
7. **It's Your Call,** Powell, Dr. Lawrence, R.
8. **It**, Groeschel, Craig
9. **Built to Last,** Collins, James, C., Porras, Jerry, I.,
10. **The Winner** Effect, Robertson, Ian, H.

11. **The 360° Leader**, Maxwell, John, C.
12. **The Power of Character in Leadership,** Munroe, Dr. Myles
13. **Who Stitched Off My Brain,** Leaf, Dr. Caroline
14. **Dare to Lead,** Brown, Brené

ENDNOTES

1. 1 Cor. 10:23
2. Prov. 25:28
3. Zheng Wang, John M. Tchernev, The "Myth" of Media Multitasking: Reciprocal Dynamics of Media Multitasking, Personal Needs, and Gratifications, *Journal of Communication*, Volume 62, Issue 3, June 2012, Pages 493–513, https://doi.org/10.1111/j.1460-2466.2012.01641.x
4. Ibid
5. Freud, S. (1923). The Ego and the Id. In J. Strachey et al. (Trans.), The Standard Edition of the Complete Psychological Works of Sigmund Freud, Volume XIX. London: Hogarth Press.
6. Ibid
7. Erikson, E. H. (1950). Childhood and society. New York, NY, US: W W Norton & Co.
8. https://www.britannica.com/biography/Jean-Piaget

9. Goleman, D. (1995). Emotional intelligence. New York, NY, England: Bantam Books, Inc.

10. Ibid

11. Julia Middleton, *Cultural Intelligence-CQ: The Competitive Edge for Leaders Crossing Borders* (Bloomsbury Publishing, London 2014)

12. Ibid.

13. Luft, J. and Ingham, H. (1955) "The Johari Window a graphic model of interpersonal awareness." *Proceedings of western training laboratory in group development,* Los Angeles:UCLA.

14. John 4:1-42

15. https://www.theatlantic.com/health/archive/2013/07/study-people-with-a-lot-of-self-control-are-happier/277349/

16. https://www.nytimes.com/interactive/2019/business/boeing-737-crashes.html

17. 2 Corinthians 7:10

18. https://www.dallasnews.com/news/crime/2013/07/20/denton-assistant-principal-who-led-secret-life-in-child-porn-world-later-committed-suicide

19. https://www.christianpost.com/news/childrens-pastor-decorated-detective-commits-suicide-after-child-porn-found-on-church-computer.html

20. *Collins, James C. (James Charles), 1958-. How The Mighty Fall:and Why Some Companies Never Give In. New York:*Jim Collins:Distributed in the U.S. and Canada exclusively by HarperCollins Publishers, 2009.

21. Matthew 6:12
22. Proverbs 23:7 (KJV)
23. https://www.huffpost.com/entry/85-of-what-we-worry-about_b_8028368
24. Habakkuk 2:2
25. Matthew 18:20
26. Hebrews 12:1
27. https://childmind.org/article/is-social-media-use-causing-depression/
28. McChesney, C., Covey, S., & Huling, J. (2012). *The 4 disciplines of execution: Achieving your wildly important goals*. London: Simon & Schuster.
29. Bruce D. Schneider, Energy Leadership: Transforming Your Workplace and Your Life From the Core (John Wiley & Sons 2010)
30. https://thei4group.com/core-energy-coaching/ and https://olivergroup.com/executive-coaching-catabolic-anabolic/
31. Schneider, *Energy Leadership*
32. https://www.bbc.com/news/business-47704987
33. https://www.washingtonpost.com/politics/2019/01/07/alexandria-ocasio-cortezs-very-bad-defense-her-falsehoods/
34. https://www.bestmattress-brand.org/pillow-personalities/
35. Sahana Singh, University of New Delhi, Quora article (need link)
36. Psalm 39

37. https://www.princeton.edu/news/2017/01/26/smart-talk-stereotypes-about-brilliance-may-set-girls-early-age-6
38. Ibid.
39. Proverbs 18:16
40. John 3:16
41. https://www.linkedin.com/pulse/people-dont-leave-bad-jobs-bosses-brigette-hyacinth/
42. Proverbs 22:1
43. Reinhold Niebuhr, *The Serenity Prayer*
44. Ecclesiastes 10:19
45. https://www.foxnews.com/lifestyle/baby-boomers-may-put-21m-homes-on-market-but-who-will-buy-them
46. https://adaa.org/about-adaa/press-room/facts-statistics
47. Ibid

FOR BOOKINGS & MORE INFORMATION VISIT:

jonathanleath.com

Made in the USA
Lexington, KY
10 December 2019